A Southern Affair to Remember

Catfish Fingers with Spicy Tartar Sauce
page 32

Crown Pork Roast with Grits Stuffing
page 200

Sweet Potato Soufflé
page 138

Corn and Okra Medley
page 122

Greens Salad with Warm Pecan Dressing
page 69

Skillet Corn Bread
page 108

Peach Cobbler
page 219

Mint Tea
page 40

Photograph of the menu items is on the title page.

3.00
m
9/11

Southern Accent
A Second Helping

Published by The Junior League of Pine Bluff, Incorporated

Copyright © 2003 by
The Junior League of Pine Bluff, Incorporated
2300 West 31st
Pine Bluff, Arkansas 71603
P. O. Box 2167
Pine Bluff, Arkansas 71613-2167
Telephone: 870-535-5027
888-568-2665 (COOK)
Fax: 870-535-0181

This cookbook is a collection of favorite recipes,
which are not necessarily original recipes.

Library of Congress Catalog Number: 2002109223
ISBN: 0-9607548-1-4

Edited, Designed, and Manufactured by
Favorite Recipes® Press
An imprint of

FRP

P. O. Box 305142
Nashville, Tennessee 37230
800-358-0560

Art Director: Steve Newman
Book Design: Starletta Polster
Project Editor: Linda A. Jones

Manufactured in the United States of America
First Printing: 2003
20,000 copies

Credits

Photography on Cover,
Title Page, Chief Saracen Mural,
The Arkansas River Mural,
The Arkansas Flag Mural
Trish Ferrell Photography

Photography of Jefferson County Courthouse
Ronnie Cates
Cates and Company Advertising

Photography of
The Governor Mike Huckabee
Delta Rivers Nature Center
Eric Maynard
Delta Rivers Nature Center

Photography of The Old Firehouse Mural
Dave Wallis
Wallis and Wallis Advertising

Historical Sidebar Photographs
Courtesy of
Lites Photography
The Lites/Wallis Collection

Graphics for Enchanted Land
of Lights and Legends
Gus VanVeckhoven
Razorback Printing

Food Stylist
Lala Treviño

Chefs/Props
Virginia Scriber, Lala Treviño, Barbara
Cash, and Jan Whitlock

Text
Ellen Burks Wyatt

Cookbook Title
Misti Smykla

Flowers
Shepherd's Florist

Legal Assistance
Cathy Lewis
Bridges, Young, Matthews & Drake PLC

Cookbook Committee
Linda Black
Barbara Cash
Mary Ann Kizer
Virginia Scriber
Lala Treviño
Jan Whitlock
Ellen Burks Wyatt

We would like to thank the
following patrons for their support:

Grand Benefactors

The Governor Mike Huckabee Delta Rivers Nature Center

Pine Bluff Convention and Visitors Bureau

Pine Bluff Festival Association

Pine Bluff National Bank

Simmons First National Bank

Grand Patron

International Paper Company

Jefferson Regional Medical Center

Preface

The Junior League of Pine Bluff, Inc., is an organization of women committed to promoting voluntarism, developing the potential of women, and improving communities through the effective action and leadership of trained volunteers. Its purpose is exclusively educational and charitable.

Pine Bluff's Junior League originated as the Junior Auxiliary in 1935. The twelve charter members of that organization focused their interest on helping children. This vision has been clear throughout the decades and is today our primary goal. We are committed volunteers improving the quality of life and the future for the children of the Pine Bluff Community.

Some of the most notable accomplishments of The Junior League of Pine Bluff include: The Sunshine School (now known as Jenkins), Volunteers in Public Schools (VIPS), Reading is Fundamental (RIF), Seabrook YMCA, Friends of the Library, Girl Scouts of America, 4-H Youth Leadership Program, Salvation Army Auxiliary, and The Little Fire House, which was the predecessor to the Arts and Science Center for Southeast Arkansas.

Ensuring the success of our educational and charitable programs requires financial contributions gained through several fund-raisers. One such fund-raiser has been our cookbook, *Southern Accent*. In 1976 The Junior League of Pine Bluff approved our first cookbook as a major fund-raiser. It has been featured in *Good Housekeeping*, inducted as a charter member into the *Southern Living*'s "Community Cookbook Hall of Fame," and has been awarded the McIlhenney Tabasco Award. The Junior League of Pine Bluff was also honored when a recipe from *Southern Accent* was included in the Association of Junior Leagues International's *The Junior League Centennial Cookbook*.

Because of the success of our first cookbook, the Junior League membership voted to publish a new cookbook. The publication of *Southern Accent, A Second Helping* marks our 30th year as a member of the Association of Junior Leagues International, Inc. The proceeds from this cookbook will enable us to continue our tradition of voluntarism in our community.

Dedication

To all the volunteers of Pine Bluff

who faithfully serve our community,

we dedicate this cookbook.

Thank you for your commitment to making

Pine Bluff the best it can be

and for making it the place you call home.

Main Street Mural

(shown on the cover)

The Main Street Mural is an actual representation of how Main

Street Pine Bluff looked in 1888. It was drawn from an old picture found

in the archives of the Jefferson County Historical Society.

This was the first mural completed and remains the most popular,

drawing tourists from around the country.

Featured in the complete mural are two town leaders, J. W. Bocage, who recorded

much of Pine Bluff's history from 1840 to 1898, and Wiley Jones (not shown),

who became one of the leading businessmen of the community.

Contents

We are pleased to include several old favorites from the original *Southern Accent*.
This symbol will signify those recipes we could not, in good conscience,
leave out of *Southern Accent, A Second Helping*.
These chosen recipes are our comfort foods from decades past and
deserve recognition in what will be our future. Enjoy!

Nutritional Guidelines

Nutritional profiles for selected recipes in *Southern Accent, A Second Helping* were provided by Lala Treviño, The Junior League of Pine Bluff, Arkansas, using the computer program MasterCook Deluxe 5.0 (Sierra Home).

MasterCook calculates the nutritional content of recipes and menus using a database of over 6,000 food items prepared using United States Department of Agriculture (USDA) publications and information from food manufacturers. More information about USDA nutritional publications can be obtained by writing:

Superintendent of Documents
U.S. Government Printing Office
Washington, D.C. 20402

As with any nutrition program, MasterCook calculates the nutritional values of recipes based on ingredients. Nutrition may vary due to how the food is prepared. For example, some foods will have a cooked value and a raw value. Be aware that there may be changes in the nutrient value during preparation that can't be easily calculated. For example, when wine is used in a recipe, the total nutritional value of the wine is added even though most of the wine will evaporate during the cooking process.

The Junior League of Pine Bluff has attempted to present these family recipes in a form that allows approximate nutritional values to be computed. Persons with dietary or health problems or whose diets require close monitoring should not rely solely on the nutritional information provided. They should consult their physicians or a registered dietitian for specific information.

Appetizers & Beverages

CHIEF SARACEN
JEFFERSON COUNTY'S LEGENDARY HERO

Chief Saracen Mural

Our Mission:
Your Satisfaction

Serving Southeast Arkansas

with Friendly,

Professional Service, and

Strong Community Support.

SPONSOR

Pine Bluff National Bank

Baked Crab Meat, Brie and Artichoke Dip

White portion of 1 medium leek, trimmed and finely chopped

1/2 cup drained canned artichoke hearts

1/2 cup thawed frozen chopped spinach

16 ounces Brie cheese

1 medium Vidalia onion or sweet onion, finely chopped

2 tablespoons minced garlic

2 tablespoons olive oil

1/4 cup riesling or other medium-dry white wine

2/3 cup heavy cream

3 tablespoons finely chopped fresh parsley

2 tablespoons finely chopped fresh dill weed

1 tablespoon finely chopped fresh tarragon

1 pound fresh jumbo lump crab meat

2 tablespoons Dijon mustard

1 tablespoon Tabasco sauce, or to taste

Salt and pepper to taste

- Rinse the leek in a large bowl of water. Remove from the water and place in a large sieve to drain. Rinse the artichoke hearts and drain. Chop the artichoke hearts finely. Squeeze the moisture from the spinach. Remove the rind from the cheese. Cut the cheese into 1/4-inch pieces.

- Sauté the leek, onion and garlic in the olive oil in a heavy skillet over medium heat until pale golden brown. Stir in the artichoke hearts and spinach. Add the wine. Cook for 3 minutes, stirring constantly. Add the cream. Simmer for 1 minute, stirring constantly. Add the cheese. Cook until the cheese begins to melt, stirring constantly. Remove from the heat. Stir in the parsley, dill weed and tarragon.

- Remove the shells from the crab meat. Combine the crab meat, Dijon mustard, Tabasco sauce, salt and pepper in a large bowl and toss to mix well. Stir in the cheese mixture. Spread evenly in a lightly oiled 11-inch gratin dish or 6-cup shallow baking dish.

- Bake at 425 degrees on the middle oven rack for 15 to 20 minutes or until golden brown. Serve with toasted thin baguette slices.

Yield: 6 to 8 servings

Hot Crab Meat, Artichoke and Jalapeño Dip

1 green bell pepper, chopped

1 tablespoon vegetable oil

2 (14-ounce) cans artichoke hearts, drained and
finely chopped

2 cups mayonnaise

1/2 cup thinly sliced scallions

1/2 cup chopped drained pimentos or roasted red bell peppers

1 cup freshly grated Parmesan cheese

1 1/2 tablespoons fresh lemon juice, or to taste

4 teaspoons Worcestershire sauce, or to taste

3 pickled jalapeño chiles, seeded and
minced, or to taste

1 teaspoon celery salt

1 pound crab meat, thawed and drained

1/3 cup sliced almonds, lightly toasted

- Sauté the bell pepper in the oil in a small heavy skillet over medium heat until softened. Remove from the heat to cool.

- Combine the bell pepper, artichokes, mayonnaise, scallions, pimentos, cheese, lemon juice, Worcestershire sauce, jalapeño chiles and celery salt in a large bowl and mix well. Stir in the crab meat gently. Spoon into a buttered ovenproof chafing dish or baking dish. Sprinkle with the almonds. (You may prepare up to this point 1 day in advance. Store, covered, in the refrigerator.)

- Bake at 375 degrees for 25 to 30 minutes or until the top is golden brown and bubbly. Serve with pita triangles or tortilla chips.

YIELD: 10 TO 14 SERVINGS

Saracen's Legend

There is a legend about one of the last of the Quapaw Indians who lived in Jefferson County. His name was Saracen. The legend says that two children were stolen from their mother in Pine Bluff by a band of Chickasaw Indians. Saracen promised the mother he would see that the children were returned safely. With that he went in search of the Chickasaws. He followed them downstream on the Arkansas River and waited until they were asleep. In the still night air he let out with the Quapaw war cry. The Chickasaws were so frightened they ran off into the night, abandoning the children. Saracen gathered them up and returned them to their mother.

Crab Meat Dip

1 1/2 cups lump crab meat, shells removed, or 2 (6-ounce) cans crab meat

2 ribs celery, finely chopped

1/2 small sweet onion, grated

1/4 cup unsweetened shredded coconut

3 tablespoons reduced-fat mayonnaise

2 tablespoons fresh lime juice

1/8 teaspoon cayenne pepper

1 teaspoon Worcestershire sauce

- Combine the crab meat, celery, onion, coconut, mayonnaise, lime juice, cayenne pepper and Worcestershire sauce in a bowl and mix well. Chill, covered, for 1 hour or longer before serving. Spoon into a 2-cup serving bowl. Serve with crisp bread or whole wheat flatbread wedges.

Note: It is also great as a spread for sandwiches.

YIELD: 8 SERVINGS

Crawfish Elegante

1 pound crawfish tails

1/4 cup (1/2 stick) margarine

1 bunch green onions, chopped

1/2 cup chopped fresh parsley

1/2 cup (1 stick) margarine

3 tablespoons flour

2 cups half-and-half

1 teaspoon Worcestershire sauce

1 teaspoon lemon juice

Salt and pepper to taste

Dash of Tabasco sauce

3 (or more) tablespoons sherry

- Blot the crawfish tails with paper towels. Sauté the crawfish tails in 1/4 cup margarine in a skillet for 10 minutes. Remove from the skillet and blot again.

- Sauté the green onions and parsley in 1/2 cup margarine in a skillet until tender. Stir in the flour and half-and-half. Cook until thickened, stirring constantly. Add the Worcestershire sauce, lemon juice, salt, pepper and Tabasco sauce and mix well. Adjust the seasonings to taste. Stir in the sherry and crawfish tails. Cook until heated through. Spoon into a chafing dish. Serve with cocktail party shells, toast rounds or crackers.

YIELD: 8 TO 10 SERVINGS

Salmon Ball

8 ounces cream cheese, softened

1 tablespoon lemon juice

2 teaspoons grated onion

1 teaspoon horseradish

2 cups canned smoked salmon

- Combine the cream cheese, lemon juice, onion, horseradish and salmon in a bowl and mix well. Shape into 1 or 2 balls.

- Serve with butter crackers or thin wheat crackers.

Note: You may roll the cheeseball(s) in 1/2 cup chopped nuts or 3 tablespoons minced fresh parsley.

YIELD: 6 TO 10 SERVINGS

Cheese and Bacon Spread

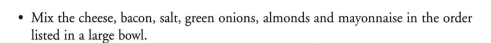

16 ounces Hoffman's super sharp soft
Cheddar cheese, grated

16 slices bacon, crisp-cooked and crumbled

1 teaspoon salt

12 green onions with tops, chopped

1 cup slivered almonds, toasted

2 cups mayonnaise

- Mix the cheese, bacon, salt, green onions, almonds and mayonnaise in the order listed in a large bowl.

- Serve on butter crackers or sesame melba rounds.

Note: You may store, covered, in the refrigerator for several days.

YIELD: 8 TO 12 SERVINGS

Confetti Dip

8 ounces Monterey Jack cheese, shredded

1 (4-ounce) can chopped green chiles

1 (4-ounce) can chopped black olives

4 green onions, chopped

1 tomato, chopped

1/4 cup minced fresh cilantro

1/2 cup Italian salad dressing

- Combine the cheese, green chiles, black olives, green onions, tomato, cilantro and salad dressing in a bowl and mix well. Chill, covered, for 8 to 12 hours. Serve with tortilla chips.

Note: This recipe may be doubled. You may substitute shredded Colby/Monterey Jack cheese.

YIELD: 8 SERVINGS

Cucumber Avocado Dip

1 tomato

2 cucumbers

2 cups sour cream

1 envelope Italian salad dressing mix

1 avocado, peeled and chopped

- Peel the tomato. Cut into halves and discard the seeds. Chop the tomato. Peel the cucumbers. Cut into halves lengthwise and discard the seeds. Chop the cucumbers. Drain the tomato and cucumbers thoroughly.

- Combine the drained tomato and cucumbers, sour cream, Italian salad dressing mix and avocado in a bowl and mix well. Chill, covered, until ready to serve.

- Serve with tortilla chips and fresh vegetables.

YIELD: 8 SERVINGS

Authentic Guacamole

2 teaspoons fresh cilantro, chopped
2 teaspoons chopped jalapeño chiles
2 tablespoons finely chopped onion

1 medium avocado, chopped
1/4 cup chopped fresh tomatoes
1/2 teaspoon salt, or to taste

• Mash 1 teaspoon of the cilantro, 1 teaspoon of the jalapeño chiles and 1 tablespoon of the onion in a mortar with a pestle.

• Add the avocado and mix well. Stir in the remaining cilantro, jalapeño chiles and onion. Add the tomatoes and salt and mix well. Serve with tortilla chips.

Note: If you like your guacamole really hot, increase the amount of jalapeño chiles.

YIELD: 4 SERVINGS

Hummus

2 cups cooked garbanzo beans
1/4 cup garbanzo bean liquid
2 tablespoons lemon juice
2 tablespoons olive oil

1/4 cup tahini
2 teaspoons minced garlic
1/2 teaspoon salt

• Process the garbanzo beans, 2 tablespoons of the garbanzo bean liquid, lemon juice and olive oil in a food processor or blender until blended, adding the remaining garbanzo bean liquid if needed for the desired consistency.

• Add the tahini, garlic and salt and blend well. The texture should be creamy and rough at the same time. Spoon into a serving bowl.

• Chill, covered, for 2 to 3 hours or longer. You may also freeze until ready to serve. Serve cold with fresh vegetables, pita bread or tortilla chips.

Note: Tahini, a sesame seed paste the consistency of peanut butter, is found at local health food stores.

YIELD: 6 TO 10 SERVINGS

Olive Spread

4 ounces mozzarella cheese, shredded

4 ounces sharp Cheddar cheese, shredded

1 (4-ounce) can chopped black olives

1 (7-ounce) jar pimento-stuffed green olives, chopped

1 bunch green onions, trimmed and chopped

1 cup mayonnaise

- Combine the mozzarella cheese, Cheddar cheese, black olives, green olives, green onions and mayonnaise in a bowl and mix well. Spoon into a large ramekin or quiche dish.

- Bake at 350 degrees for 20 minutes or until hot and bubbly. Serve with crackers.

YIELD: 10 TO 12 SERVINGS

Hot Onion Soufflé

2 (10-ounce) packages frozen chopped onions, thawed

24 ounces cream cheese, softened

2 cups grated Parmesan cheese

1/2 cup mayonnaise

- Roll the thawed onions in paper towels, squeezing to remove the excess moisture. Combine the onions, cream cheese, Parmesan cheese and mayonnaise in a bowl and mix well. Spoon into a shallow 2-quart soufflé dish.

- Bake at 425 degrees for 15 to 20 minutes or until golden brown. Serve with corn chips or assorted crackers.

Note: You may double the recipe. This recipe freezes well.

YIELD: 6 CUPS

Party Cheese Dip

2 tablespoons minced onion
1 tablespoon butter
2 pounds ground beef
32 ounces Cheddar cheese, shredded
2 tablespoons garlic powder

1 1/2 (10-ounce) cans tomatoes with
green chiles
1 cup vermouth
Salt and pepper to taste

- Sauté the onion in the butter in a small skillet until translucent.

- Brown the ground beef in a large skillet, stirring until crumbly; drain. Add the sautéed onion, cheese, garlic powder, tomatoes with green chiles, vermouth, salt and pepper and mix well. Cook until the cheese melts, stirring constantly. Spoon into a chafing dish.

- Serve with tortilla chips.

Note: You may substitute 16 ounces American cheese and 16 ounces Velveeta cheese for the Cheddar cheese.

YIELD: 12 TO 15 SERVINGS

Pizza Dip

8 ounces cream cheese, softened
1 (16-ounce) jar pizza sauce
1/2 cup chopped green onions
1/4 cup chopped green bell pepper

2 cups (8 ounces) shredded mozzarella
cheese
1/2 cup chopped black olives
1 (3-ounce) package sliced pepperoni

- Press the cream cheese in the bottom of a greased 9-inch pie plate. Spread with the pizza sauce. Layer the green onions, bell pepper, mozzarella cheese, olives and pepperoni in the order listed over the pizza sauce.

- Bake at 350 degrees for 20 minutes. Serve with tortilla chips.

YIELD: 10 TO 12 SERVINGS

Sun-Dried Tomato Dip

6 sun-dried tomato halves
2 garlic cloves
8 ounces cream cheese
1 cup sour cream
1 tablespoon horseradish
1 large bunch basil, trimmed
Juice of 1 lemon, strained
Salt and pepper to taste

- Place the sun-dried tomatoes in water to cover in a bowl. Cover with plastic wrap. Microwave on High for 1 minute. Let stand, covered, until cool. Drain and pat dry.

- Process the tomatoes and garlic in a food processor to form a paste. Add the cream cheese and pulse until smooth. Add the sour cream, horseradish, basil and lemon juice and pulse until the basil is finely chopped and mixed evenly throughout. Adjust the seasonings. Season with salt and pepper to taste.

Note: You'll eat it on everything—from chips and vegetables to bagels, pasta and sandwiches. Beware it's addictive. This dip stores well and can be easily doubled.

YIELD: ABOUT 3 CUPS

Oven "Sun-Dried" Tomatoes
This is how you can "sun-dry" tomatoes in the privacy of your own kitchen. Set your oven to its lowest setting (below 200 degrees). Cut Italian-style tomatoes (such as Roma or plum) into halves from top to bottom. Scoop out the seeds using your fingers. Place the tomatoes cut side down directly on the oven racks. Bake for 12 to 15 hours or until the tomatoes are dry. A good way to do this is to place the tomatoes in the oven and let them bake all night.

Black Bean Salsa

2 (15-ounce) cans black beans, rinsed and drained

1 (10-ounce) can tomatoes with green chiles

1 (4-ounce) can green chiles

1 cup salsa

5 green onions, chopped

2 tablespoons fresh cilantro, chopped, or 1 tablespoon dried cilantro

• Combine the black beans, tomatoes with green chiles, green chiles, salsa, green onions and cilantro in a bowl and mix well. Chill, covered, for 1 to 2 hours or until ready to serve. Serve with corn chips.

Note: You may also serve over lettuce as a dinner salad. You may also add one 11-ounce can white Shoe Peg corn.

YIELD: 8 SERVINGS

Salsa Fresca

6 medium tomatoes, seeded and finely chopped

1 red onion, finely chopped

2 garlic cloves, minced

1 fresh green chile, seeded and finely chopped

1 tablespoon fresh lime juice

2 tablespoons olive oil

2 tablespoons finely chopped fresh cilantro

Salt and pepper to taste

• Combine the tomatoes, onion, garlic, green chile, lime juice, olive oil and cilantro in a bowl and mix well. Add salt and pepper. Cover and let stand at room temperature for 30 minutes to allow the flavors to blend. Serve at room temperature or chill for 8 to 12 hours before serving.

YIELD: 1 2/3 CUPS

Tuscon Black and White Bean Salsa

1 (11-ounce) can white Shoe Peg corn, drained

3 tablespoons vegetable oil

1 (16-ounce) can black beans, rinsed and drained

1 (15-ounce) can Northern beans, rinsed and drained

1 cup chopped red bell pepper

1/2 cup chopped red onion

2 tablespoons chopped jalapeño chiles, or to taste

2 tablespoons lime juice

3 garlic cloves, minced

1 teaspoon oregano

1 tablespoon chili powder

1 1/2 teaspoons cumin

Salt and pepper to taste

- Sauté the corn in 1 tablespoon of the oil in a small skillet until light brown. Remove from the heat.

- Combine the remaining oil, black beans, Northern beans, bell pepper, onion, jalapeño chiles, lime juice, garlic, oregano, chili powder and cumin in a large bowl and mix well. Stir in the sautéed corn. Season with salt and pepper to taste.

- Serve with tortilla chips.

YIELD: 10 TO 12 SERVINGS

Saracen's Final Resting Place

When the Quapaws moved to Oklahoma in 1833, Saracen did not wish to go. His petition to stay was granted and he spent his final days on the banks of the Arkansas River. In the early 1880s the Bureau of Ethnology wanted to dig up Saracen's body and take it to Washington, D.C. But the townspeople who regarded him so highly, refused to reveal Saracen's true resting place. Today, Saracen's grave can be visited in the St. Joseph's Catholic Cemetery. Visitors come from all over to see his tombstone.

Authentic Buffalo Wings

3 pounds chicken wings	1 cup Frank's hot sauce
Vegetable oil for deep-frying	2½ teaspoons Tabasco sauce
¼ cup (½ stick) butter	2½ teaspoons cayenne pepper

- Disjoint the chicken wings and discard the tips. Deep-fry in 425-degree oil in a deep fryer for 15 to 25 minutes or until crispy and cooked through. Drain on paper towels.

- Melt the butter in a saucepan. Add the hot sauce, Tabasco sauce and cayenne pepper and mix well. Place the chicken wings in a container with a tight-fitting lid. Add the sauce mixture. Seal the container with the lid and shake to coat well. Serve hot.

YIELD: 8 TO 10 SERVINGS

Crab Meat-Stuffed Mushrooms

1 (16-ounce) package imitation crab meat	1¼ cups seasoned bread crumbs
16 ounces Pepper Jack cheese	10 tablespoons unsalted butter, melted
Bulbs from 1 bunch green onions	8 containers large whole mushrooms
Leaves from ⅓ bunch fresh parsley	¼ cup (½ stick) unsalted butter, melted

- Process the imitation crab meat, cheese, green onion bulbs and parsley in a food processor until shredded. Combine with the bread crumbs and 10 tablespoons butter in a large bowl and squeeze with hands to mix well.

- Remove the mushroom stems, reserving the caps. Rinse the reserved caps to clean. Stuff the crab meat mixture into the caps. Arrange in an ungreased baking pan. Pour ¼ cup butter over the stuffed mushroom caps. Bake at 350 degrees for 20 to 30 minutes or until heated through.

Note: You may store any unused crab meat stuffing in the freezer.

YIELD: ABOUT 30 SERVINGS

Italian Stuffed Mushrooms

1/2 cup butter cracker crumbs

1/3 cup chicken broth

2 tablespoons butter, melted

1 medium onion

1 small garlic clove, minced

3 tablespoons grated Parmesan cheese

2 ounces pepperoni, ground

1 tablespoon parsley

1/4 teaspoon oregano

1/2 teaspoon seasoned salt

5 quarts mushrooms

- Combine the cracker crumbs, broth, butter, onion, garlic, cheese, pepperoni, parsley, oregano and seasoned salt in a bowl and mix well.

- Remove the stems from the mushrooms, reserving the caps. Stuff a small amount of the pepperoni mixture into each cap. Arrange on a baking sheet.

- Bake at 325 degrees for 25 minutes.

YIELD: ABOUT 30 SERVINGS

Almond-Stuffed Dates

Cut 25 slices of bacon into halves. Stuff 50 whole almonds into 50 pitted dates. Wrap the bacon halves around each, securing with a wooden pick. Arrange on a baking sheet. Bake at 400 degrees for 12 to 15 minutes or until the bacon is cooked through.

Note: This was served at Charity Ball 1999.

Spinach Balls

2 (10-ounce) packages frozen spinach

2 cups seasoned bread crumbs

1 large onion, minced

6 eggs, beaten

3/4 cup (1 1/2 sticks) butter, melted

1 cup grated Parmesan cheese

1 teaspoon garlic salt

1 teaspoon pepper

1 teaspoon MSG

- Cook the spinach using the package directions; drain well. Combine the spinach, bread crumbs, onion, eggs, butter, cheese, garlic salt, pepper and MSG in a bowl and mix well.

- Shape by rounded tablespoonfuls into balls. Arrange on a nonstick baking sheet.

- Bake at 350 degrees for 15 to 20 minutes or until golden brown.

Note: You may prepare ahead and store in the freezer before baking.

YIELD: 100 BALLS

Sausage Dip

Brown 1 pound sausage in a skillet, stirring until crumbly; drain. Squeeze out any excess grease with a paper towel. Add 8 ounces softened cream cheese and one 10-ounce can tomatoes with green chiles. Heat until the cream cheese is melted, stirring constantly. Serve immediately with tortilla chips or corn chips.

Note: For a spicier taste use hot sausage. You may also double or triple the recipe.

Three-Pepper Tortilla Rolls

1 cup green bell pepper strips
1 cup red bell pepper strips
1 cup yellow bell pepper strips
1/2 cup thin onion slices
1/3 cup margarine
1/2 teaspoon cumin
8 ounces cream cheese, softened
8 ounces sharp Cheddar cheese, shredded
1/2 cup grated Parmesan cheese
10 (6-inch) flour tortillas

- Sauté the bell pepper strips and onion slices in the margarine in a large skillet until softened. Stir in the cumin. Drain, reserving the liquid.

- Beat the cream cheese, Cheddar cheese and Parmesan cheese at medium speed in a small mixing bowl until blended. Add enough of the reserved liquid to make the desired spreading consistency.

- Spoon 2 tablespoons of the cheese mixture onto each tortilla. Top with the bell pepper mixture and roll up. Cut each tortilla into 4 slices and secure with wooden picks. Arrange on a baking sheet.

- Bake at 425 degrees for 8 to 10 minutes.

Note: This was served at Charity Ball 1999.

YIELD: 40 SERVINGS

Miniature Beef Wellingtons

7 ounces frozen all-butter puff pastry, thawed

1/3 cup boursin cheese, at room temperature

8 ounces beef tenderloin, trimmed and cut into 1/2-inch cubes

Salt and freshly ground pepper to taste

1 egg, lightly beaten

- Roll the puff pastry into a 15×17 1/2-inch rectangle on a lightly floured sheet of parchment paper. Cut into 1 1/2-inch squares. Spoon a scant 1/4 teaspoon cheese in the center of each square.

- Season the beef with salt and pepper. Place 1 beef cube on the cheese in each square. Fold the pastry over the beef, neatly tucking in the corners. Arrange seam side down on a large baking sheet lined with parchment paper. Brush lightly with the egg.

- Bake at 400 degrees for 10 to 12 minutes or until puffed and golden brown. Serve hot on a large serving platter.

Note: You may prepare ahead and store in the freezer before baking.

YIELD: 10 TO 12 SERVINGS

Pepperoni Squares

2 cups flour

2 eggs

1 teaspoon salt

$^1/_2$ teaspoon oregano

12 ounces Cheddar cheese, shredded

1$^1/_2$ cups milk

1 package sliced pepperoni

$^1/_4$ cup grated Parmesan cheese

- Combine the flour, eggs, salt, oregano, Cheddar cheese and milk in a bowl and mix well. Stir in the pepperoni.

- Pour into a greased 9×13-inch baking pan. Sprinkle with the Parmesan cheese.

- Bake at 350 degrees for 35 to 40 minutes or until golden brown. Remove from the oven to cool. Cut into squares.

Note: Great served with pizza sauce.

YIELD: 12 SERVINGS

Chicken Bites

8 ounces cream cheese, softened

1/2 teaspoon lemon juice

1/2 teaspoon basil

1/4 teaspoon onion salt

1/8 teaspoon oregano

1/8 teaspoon thyme

1 cup finely chopped cooked chicken

1/2 cup finely chopped celery

1 (2-ounce) jar diced pimento, drained

2 (8-count) cans crescent rolls

1 egg, lightly beaten

1 1/2 teaspoons sesame seeds

- Mix the cream cheese, lemon juice, basil, onion salt, oregano and thyme in a small bowl. Combine the chicken, celery and pimento in a large bowl and mix well. Add the cream cheese mixture and stir to mix well.

- Separate the crescent roll dough into 8 rectangles, pressing the perforations to seal. Spread 1/4 cup of the chicken mixture on each rectangle, leaving 1/2-inch margin on each long side. Roll up, beginning at the long sides and pinching the edges to seal. Brush with the egg. Sprinkle with the sesame seeds. Cut each roll-up into 5 pieces. Arrange seam side down on a baking sheet.

- Bake at 350 degrees for 12 to 15 minutes or until brown.

Note: You may prepare ahead by arranging on a baking sheet and freezing for 1 hour. Place in a sealable freezer bag and store in the freezer until ready to serve. To serve, place seam side down on a baking sheet. Let stand for 30 minutes to thaw. Bake at 350 degrees for 12 to 15 minutes or until golden brown. Serve warm.

MAKES 40 PIECES

Toasted Pecans

Toss 4 cups pecan halves in 1/4 cup (1/2 stick) melted butter, margarine or vegetable oil in a bowl. Arrange in a single layer on a baking sheet. Sprinkle lightly with salt or garlic salt to taste. Bake at 300 degrees for 15 to 20 minutes. Remove from the oven. Blot with paper towels if the pecans seem too greasy and sprinkle with salt if needed. Let stand until cool. Store in an airtight container.

Caviar Roulade

1/4 cup (1/2 stick) butter
1/2 cup flour, sifted
2 cups milk
4 egg yolks, beaten
4 egg whites, stiffly beaten
6 ounces cream cheese, softened
3 tablespoons sour cream
4 ounces black caviar
1 1/2 cups sour cream

- Grease a 10×15-inch baking pan. Line with waxed paper. Grease and flour the waxed paper.

- Melt the butter in a saucepan. Stir in the flour gradually. Cook until bubbly, whisking constantly. Add the milk gradually, stirring constantly. Bring to a boil and reduce the heat. Simmer for 1 minute. Remove from the heat.

- Stir a small amount of the hot mixture into the beaten egg yolks in a bowl. Add the egg yolks to the hot mixture and mix well. Fold in the stiffly beaten egg whites. Pour into the prepared pan.

- Bake at 325 degrees on the lower oven rack for 40 minutes or until the top is brown. Remove from the oven and invert carefully onto waxed paper.

- Combine the cream cheese, 3 tablespoons sour cream and 2 ounces of the caviar in a bowl and mix gently. Spread over the cake. Roll up as for a jelly roll.

- Combine 1 1/2 cups sour cream and remaining 2 ounces caviar in a bowl and mix well.

- To serve, cut the roulade into slices. Top with the caviar sauce.

Note: You may prepare 1 day ahead and store, covered, in the refrigerator. This recipe is fabulous and elegant for a cocktail party. It is great even if you do not like caviar.

YIELD: 8 SERVINGS

Catfish Fingers with Spicy Tartar Sauce

1¹/2 cups dry bread crumbs
1/4 cup grated Parmesan cheese
1 teaspoon Cajun seasoning
1 egg

1/4 cup milk
1 pound catfish fillets, cut into
1-inch strips
Spicy Tartar Sauce (below)

- Mix the bread crumbs, cheese and Cajun seasoning in a shallow dish. Beat the egg and milk in a bowl. Dip the fish in the egg mixture; dredge in the crumb mixture. Arrange in a single layer on a greased baking sheet.
- Bake at 350 degrees for 15 minutes. Serve with Spicy Tartar Sauce.

YIELD: 8 SERVINGS

Per Serving (excluding unknown items): 159 Calories; 4 g Fat (24.7% calories from fat); 14 g Protein; 15 g Carbohydrate; 59 mg Cholesterol; 283 mg Sodium. Exchanges: 1 Grain (Starch); 1¹/2 Lean Meat; 0 Non-Fat Milk; 1/2 Fat; 0 Other Carbohydrates.

Spicy Tartar Sauce

1/2 cup mayonnaise
1 cup sour cream
1 teaspoon fresh lemon juice
2 tablespoons finely chopped
green onions

2 teaspoons fresh parsley, chopped
3/4 teaspoon red pepper
2 teaspoons sweet pickle relish
(optional)
Salt and pepper to taste

- Combine the mayonnaise, sour cream and lemon juice in a bowl and blend well. Add the green onions, parsley, red pepper, relish, salt and pepper and stir gently to mix. Chill, covered, until ready to serve.

YIELD: 8 SERVINGS

Per serving (excluding unknown items): 163 Calories; 18 g Fat (93.1% calories from fat); 1 g Protein; 2 g Carbohydrate; 18 mg Cholesterol; 104 mg Sodium. Exchanges: 0 Grain (Starch); 0 Vegetable; 0 Fruit; 0 Non-Fat Milk; 2 Fat; 0 Other Carbohydrates.
Nutritional analysis includes the optional ingredient.

Miniature Salmon Cakes

1 (16-ounce) can pink salmon
1 egg
1/3 cup finely chopped onion
1/2 cup self-rising flour
Vegetable oil for frying

- Drain the salmon, reserving 2 tablespoons of the liquid. Remove the bones from the salmon. Combine the salmon, egg, onion, flour and reserved liquid in a bowl and mix well. Shape into small patties.

- Fry in hot oil in a skillet for 5 minutes or until golden brown. Serve with tartar sauce or ketchup.

YIELD: 4 TO 6 SERVINGS

Cotton Blossoms

16 ounces cream cheese, softened
1 (8-ounce) package imitation crab meat
1 (12-ounce) package won ton wrappers
Vegetable oil for deep-frying
1/4 cup (1/2 stick) butter
1 (12-ounce) jar apricot preserves
1 to 2 teaspoons ground nutmeg

- Combine the cream cheese and imitation crab meat in a bowl and mix well. Drop by spoonfuls onto each won ton wrapper and pinch the edges to seal.

- Deep-fry in batches in hot oil in a deep fryer for 10 to 12 seconds or until the edges are light golden brown. Do not overcook. Remove to paper towels to drain.

- Melt the butter in a saucepan. Add the preserves and nutmeg and mix well. Serve the won tons with the apricot sauce.

Note: Do not use fat-free cream cheese in this recipe.

YIELD: 50 SERVINGS

Oysters Belgique

2 to 3 (12-ounce) containers oysters

8 ounces fresh or frozen small shrimp

2 tablespoons butter

Milk

2 tablespoons dry white wine or
dry vermouth

1/4 cup (1/2 stick) butter

3 tablespoons flour

1 egg yolk

Salt and white pepper to taste

Bread crumbs to taste

Shredded Swiss cheese to taste

- Drain the oysters, reserving the liquor. Peel the shrimp and devein. Rinse under cold water and pat dry. Chop the shrimp coarsely.

- Melt 2 tablespoons butter in a small saucepan. Heat until the foam from the butter begins to subside. Stir in the shrimp. Cook over medium heat for 2 to 3 minutes, stirring constantly.

- Pour the reserved liquor into a glass measure. Add enough milk to measure 1 3/4 cups. Stir in the wine. Melt 1/4 cup butter in a heavy saucepan. Do not brown. Whisk in 3 tablespoons flour. Add the milk mixture, whisking constantly. Bring to a boil over medium-high heat and reduce the heat. Simmer for 3 minutes.

- Beat the egg yolk in a bowl. Stir a small amount of the hot sauce into the beaten egg yolk. Stir the egg yolk into the hot sauce. Season with salt and white pepper. Stir in the shrimp.

- Arrange clean sea shells or small ramekins in a shallow baking pan, using rock salt to stabilize the shells if needed. Add 1 tablespoon sauce to each shell. Add the oysters. Top with more sauce. Place on an oven rack in the upper third of the oven.

- Bake at 400 degrees for 8 minutes. Sprinkle with bread crumbs and cheese. Cook for 3 minutes.

Note: In memory of Dr. Sam Harris.

Yield: 10 to 12 servings

Scallops Baked in Phyllo with Lemon Butter

1 tablespoon butter	1 tablespoon brandy (optional)
2 tablespoons minced shallots	1 teaspoon minced fresh marjoram, or
1/2 cup dry white wine	1/4 teaspoon dried marjoram
2 tablespoons whipping cream	Salt and pepper to taste
6 phyllo sheets	1 egg yolk
1/2 cup (1 stick) butter, melted	5 tablespoons butter
8 large sea scallops	1 1/2 tablespoons fresh lemon juice

- Melt 1 tablespoon butter in a small heavy saucepan over medium heat. Add the shallots. Sauté for 3 minutes. Add the wine. Boil for 5 minutes or until the liquid is reduced to 1/4 cup. Stir in the cream.

- Stack 3 phyllo sheets on top of each other, brushing each layer with the melted butter and keeping the remaining sheets covered to prevent drying out. Cut the phyllo stack into four 6-inch squares. Place 1 scallop in the center of each square. Brush with brandy and sprinkle with marjoram. Season with salt and pepper. Bring up the sides of phyllo around the scallops to form pouches and pinch the centers to seal. Repeat the process with the remaining phyllo sheets, melted butter, scallops, brandy and marjoram. Arrange the pouches on a baking sheet. Brush with melted butter. (The sauce and phyllo pouches can be made up to 4 hours ahead. Cover separately and chill in the refrigerator.)

- Bake at 425 degrees for 10 minutes or until golden brown. Heat the sauce over medium-low heat. Whisk in the egg yolk. Do not boil. Add 5 tablespoons butter. Heat until the butter melts, whisking constantly. Add the lemon juice. Season with salt and pepper. Spoon the sauce onto 4 serving plates. Top each with 2 phyllo pouches.

YIELD: 4 SERVINGS

Crab Meat Bites

1/2 cup (1 stick) butter, softened
2 tablespoons mayonnaise
1 (4-ounce) can crab meat, drained
1 (5-ounce) jar Old English
cheese spread

1/2 to 1 teaspoon minced garlic
Dash of cayenne pepper
Dash of Worcestershire sauce
1 package English muffins, split
Paprika to taste

• Combine the butter, mayonnaise, crab meat, cheese spread, garlic, cayenne pepper and Worcestershire sauce in a bowl and mix well. Spread generously on each muffin half. Cut each half into 6 wedges. Arrange on a baking sheet. Freeze until firm. Place in sealable freezer bags and seal. Store in the freezer until ready to serve.

• To serve, arrange on a baking sheet. Bake at 350 degrees for 20 minutes. Sprinkle with paprika.

YIELD: 12 SERVINGS

Swiss Shrimp Bites

1 cup shrimp, cut into small pieces
1/4 cup chopped green onions
1 teaspoon lemon juice
1 cup (4 ounces) shredded Swiss cheese
1/2 cup mayonnaise

1/4 teaspoon curry powder
30 miniature phyllo shells, at room
temperature
30 water chestnut slices
Paprika to taste

• Combine the shrimp, green onions, lemon juice, cheese, mayonnaise and curry powder in a bowl and mix well. Spoon into the phyllo shells. Top each with a water chestnut. Sprinkle with paprika. Arrange on a baking sheet.

• Bake at 350 degrees for 8 minutes or until the filling is hot. Serve immediately.

YIELD: 30 SERVINGS

Marinated Shrimp and Tortellini

1 1/2 cups olive oil

1/2 cup white vinegar

2/3 cup ketchup

1 tablespoon Dijon mustard

1 tablespoon lemon juice

5 teaspoons horseradish

5 garlic cloves, minced

1 teaspoon hot pepper sauce

1 teaspoon salt

1 teaspoon pepper

1/2 cup chopped celery

3 pounds medium shrimp, cooked and peeled

16 ounces cheese-filled tortellini, cooked and drained

- Whisk the olive oil, vinegar, ketchup, Dijon mustard, lemon juice, horseradish, garlic, hot pepper sauce, salt and pepper in a bowl until smooth.

- Combine the celery, shrimp and pasta in a large bowl. Add the marinade and toss gently to coat. Chill, covered, for 24 hours.

Note: For variation in color, use cheese-filled spinach tortellini.

YIELD: 10 TO 12 SERVINGS

Creole Coffee

This will be popular even with folks who think they don't like coffee.

6 cups brewed strong French roast coffee or chicory
1 cinnamon stick
3 tablespoons sugar
6 tablespoons (heaping) International Foods Café Français mix
6 tablespoons brandy

• Combine the coffee, cinnamon stick, sugar, Café Français mix and brandy in a coffee pot. Steep for 30 minutes or longer. Serve in demitasse cups or punch cups.

Note: For a coffee pot that holds 30 to 35 cups of brewed coffee, use 1 container Café Français, 3/4 cup sugar, 1 cup brandy and 3 cinnamon sticks.

YIELD: 6 CUPS

Hot Cranberry Drink

2 quarts cranberry juice cocktail
2 cups orange juice
1 cup pineapple juice
3 tablespoons lemon juice
1 cup sugar
3 cinnamon sticks

• Combine the cranberry juice cocktail, orange juice, pineapple juice, lemon juice, sugar and cinnamon sticks in a large coffee pot and mix well. Heat until hot.

Note: You may use cranapple or crangrape juice cocktail.

YIELD: 10 TO 12 SERVINGS

Fruit Tea

3 lemons

2 oranges

8 cups (2 quarts) water

9 (family-size) tea bags

1 cup chopped fresh mint leaves

3 cups sugar

1/4 cup maraschino cherry juice

6 cups (1 1/2 quarts) cold water

- Squeeze the juice from the lemons and oranges into a small pitcher, reserving the lemons. Chill the juice, covered, in the refrigerator.

- Bring 8 cups water to a boil in a saucepan. Remove from the heat. Add the tea bags, mint leaves and reserved lemons. Steep for 30 minutes. Strain into a large pitcher, discarding the solids. Stir in the sugar until dissolved. Chill for 24 hours.

- Add the juice mixture and cherry juice. Stir in 6 cups cold water. Garnish each serving with fresh mint and a maraschino cherry.

YIELD: 1 GALLON

The Battle of Pine Bluff

The Union army occupied Pine Bluff from September 14, 1863, until the end of the Civil War. Although the Union's position in Pine Bluff is said to have been amicable, a brief battle took place on October 25, 1863, between 2,500 Confederate troops led by Brigadier General John S. Marmaduke and the 550 Union troops led by Colonel Powell Clayton. The Confederate troops were withdrawn and Pine Bluff was occupied by the United States Army until the end of the war. As a part of the bicentennial celebration in Jefferson County, a marker commemorating this battle was placed on the west side of the Jefferson County Courthouse.

Mint Tea

3 (family-size) tea bags
Leaves from 6 large mint sprigs
1¹/2 cups boiling water
1 cup sugar

1¹/2 cups boiling water
¹/2 cup lemon juice
4 cups (1 quart) cold water

- Steep the tea bags and mint leaves in 1¹/2 cups boiling water in a small pitcher for 15 minutes. Dissolve the sugar in 1¹/2 cups boiling water in a large pitcher. Stir in the lemon juice. Strain the tea, discarding the solids. Pour into the lemon mixture. Add 4 cups cold water and mix well. Chill, covered, until ready to serve.

- To serve, pour over ice in glasses and garnish with sprigs of fresh mint and lemon slices.

Note: This recipe may be doubled.

YIELD: 2 QUARTS

Spiced Tea

2 cups water
1¹/2 sticks cinnamon, broken
1 teaspoon whole cloves
3 (1-serving size) tea bags

2¹/2 cups sugar
2 cups strained orange juice
¹/2 cup strained lemon juice
10 cups (2¹/2 quarts) water

- Bring 2 cups water, cinnamon sticks and cloves to a boil in a saucepan and reduce the heat. Simmer for 5 minutes. Remove from the heat. Add the tea bags. Steep for 5 minutes. Strain the tea, discarding the solids. Return to the saucepan. Add the sugar and stir until dissolved. Add the orange juice, lemon juice and 10 cups water and blend well. Heat to serving temperature.

Note: Do not use ground cinnamon and ground cloves as they cannot be strained and will leave a sediment.

YIELD: 20 SERVINGS

Piña Colada Sherbet Drink

1 cup pineapple sherbet

8 ounces ice

2 tablespoons pineapple juice

2 tablespoons cream of coconut

1 tablespoon cream

2 tablespoons rum (optional)

- Combine the sherbet, ice, pineapple juice, cream of coconut, cream and rum in the order listed in a blender. Process at high speed for 2 minutes.

YIELD: 2 SERVINGS

Citrus Punch

2 cups sugar

2^1/$_2$ cups water

1 cup lemon juice

1 cup orange juice with pulp

1 (6-ounce) can frozen pineapple juice concentrate

4 cups (1 quart) ginger ale

- Bring the sugar and water to a boil in a saucepan. Boil for 10 minutes. Remove from the heat. Add the lemon juice, orange juice and pineapple juice concentrate and blend well.

- Chill, covered, in the refrigerator until ready to serve.

- To serve, stir in the ginger ale. Pour into a punch bowl. Garnish with cherries frozen in orange juice cubes.

YIELD: 16 TO 20 SERVINGS

Rum Punch

1 (46-ounce) can orange juice

1 (46-ounce) can pineapple juice

2 (11-ounce) cans apricot nectar

1 (10-ounce) jar maraschino cherries

1 (8-ounce) can crushed pineapple

1 (750-milliliter) bottle rum, or to taste

- Combine the orange juice, pineapple juice, apricot nectar, maraschino cherries, pineapple and rum in a punch bowl and mix well.

- Garnish with orange slices. Serve over ice.

YIELD: 15 TO 20 SERVINGS

Ruby Red Wine Punch

1 bottle red wine, such as claret or burgundy, chilled

3 cups orange juice, chilled

1/3 cup lemon juice

1/2 cup sugar

4 cups (1 quart) ginger ale, chilled

- Combine the wine, orange juice, lemon juice and sugar in a punch bowl and mix well.

- Add the ginger ale just before serving.

YIELD: 12 TO 15 SERVINGS

Irish Cream

1 cup light cream
1 (14-ounce) can sweetened condensed milk
1²/3 cups Irish whiskey
1 teaspoon instant coffee granules
2 tablespoons chocolate syrup
1 teaspoon vanilla extract
1 teaspoon almond extract

- Combine the cream, condensed milk, whiskey, coffee granules, chocolate syrup, vanilla extract and almond extract in a blender. Process at high speed for 30 seconds.

- Store in a tightly covered container in the refrigerator for at least 2 months. Be sure and shake the container well before serving.

Note: Wonderful in coffee.

YIELD: 4 CUPS

Wine Ice Cubes

Don't waste that leftover wine from your dinner party. Pour the wine into ice cube trays and freeze to use for future sauces and such.

White Sangria

Fruit, such as white grapes and green apples, or orange and lemon slices
1/3 cup Cointreau
1 (750-milliliter) bottle dry white wine, chilled
1 (10-ounce) bottle bitter lemon

• Soak the fruit in the liqueur in a large pitcher. Add the wine and stir to mix well. Stir in the bitter lemon.

Note: You may substitute a mixture of two 10-ounce bottles club soda and juice from 1 lemon for the bitter lemon.

YIELD: 8 TO 10 SERVINGS

Banana Strawberry Smoothie

1 medium banana, sliced and frozen
1 cup strawberry halves, frozen
1/4 cup frozen orange juice concentrate
1 1/2 cups skim milk
1/4 teaspoon almond extract

• Process the banana, strawberries, orange juice concentrate, milk and almond extract in a blender until smooth, stopping to scrape the side as needed. Serve immediately.

YIELD: 2 SERVINGS

Per Serving (excluding unknown items): 198 Calories; 1 g Fat (4.1% calories from fat); 8 g Protein; 41 g Carbohydrate; 3 mg Cholesterol; 97 mg Sodium. Exchanges: 2 Fruit; 1/2 Non-Fat Milk.

Soups, Sandwiches & Salads

The Arkansas Flag Mural—Willie Kavanaugh Hocker

The Murals of Pine Bluff

In an effort to raise pride in the Pine Bluff community, a group of dedicated citizens approached Pine Bluff Development, Inc., about a beautification project involving historic murals. So far, thirteen murals have been completed and another nine will complete the project. The murals depict Pine Bluff's rich history, using actual photographs to guide nationally known artists in their painting. The most popular mural to date is the mural pictured on the cover of our cookbook, which shows Main Street in the year 1888. A park was constructed around this mural and is a popular tourist stop for visitors.

SPONSOR

Curried Butternut Squash and Apple Soup

2 pounds butternut squash

1/2 cup chopped onion

2 small ribs celery, chopped

2 McIntosh apples, peeled, cored and chopped

2 tablespoons unsalted butter

Salt and pepper to taste

1 tablespoon curry powder

4 cups chicken stock or broth

1 bay leaf

1 cup heavy cream or half-and-half

Lemon juice to taste

- Place the squash on a lightly oiled baking sheet. Bake at 375 degrees on the middle oven rack for 30 to 35 minutes or until tender. Remove from the oven to cool. Peel the squash and remove the seeds. Cut into small pieces. Place in a bowl and cover.

- Combine the onion, celery, apples, butter, salt and pepper in a saucepan. Cover with a buttered circle of waxed paper and the lid. Cook over medium heat for 5 minutes, stirring occasionally. Stir in the curry powder. Cook over medium-low heat for 3 minutes, stirring constantly. Add the chicken stock and bay leaf. Simmer for 30 minutes. Discard the bay leaf.

- Purée the mixture in batches alternately with the squash in a food processor fitted with a steel blade. Force through a food mill into a stainless steel or enameled saucepan. Add the cream and lemon juice. Season with salt and pepper. Bring to a simmer over medium heat. Do not boil. Ladle into heated soup bowls.

YIELD: 6 TO 8 SERVINGS

Strawberry Soup

1 cup fresh or frozen strawberries,
crushed or sliced
1 cup sugar
1 cup sour cream
4 cups (1 quart) half-and-half
1 teaspoon lemon juice

- Beat the strawberries, sugar and sour cream at low speed in a mixing bowl until well-mixed. Stir in the half-and-half and lemon juice.
- Chill, covered, until ready to serve.

YIELD: 4 TO 6 SERVINGS

Broccoli Cheese Soup

1 large onion, chopped
3 tablespoons margarine
2 (10-ounce) packages frozen chopped broccoli
2 (10-ounce) cans cream of chicken soup
1 (10-ounce) can cream of celery soup
3 1/2 soup cans milk
1 (8-ounce) jar Cheez Whiz

- Sauté the onion in the margarine in a large saucepan until translucent. Add the broccoli, chicken soup, celery soup, milk and Cheez Whiz.
- Simmer for 30 minutes. Ladle into soup bowls.

YIELD: 4 SERVINGS

Adoption of the Arkansas Flag

In 1912, when the United States Navy launched one of its new battleships and named it the USS Arkansas, the Navy asked for the State flag to be displayed on the battlewagon. At that time Arkansas did not have a state flag. The Pine Bluff Chapter of the Daughters of the American Revolution decided to rectify the situation by designing a state flag. Miss Willie Hocker sketched out the design and it was then fashioned out of silk. It was unanimously adopted by the Arkansas Legislature on February 18, 1913.

Smoked Gouda Cheese Soup

1/4 cup (1/2 stick) butter

1/4 cup flour

2 cups half-and-half

2 cups milk

2 cups (16 ounces) shredded Gouda cheese

1 teaspoon Worcestershire sauce

1/4 teaspoon red pepper

2 or 3 drops of Tabasco sauce

Salt to taste

Paprika to taste

• Melt the butter in a large saucepan over medium-low heat. Stir in the flour. Cook for 1 minute, stirring constantly. Stir in the half-and-half and milk gradually.

• Cook over medium-low heat until slightly thickened, stirring constantly. Pour into a blender. Add the cheese. Process until foamy. Return to the saucepan.

• Cook over medium-low heat until heated through. Stir in the Worcestershire sauce, red pepper, Tabasco sauce and salt. Ladle into soup bowls. Sprinkle with paprika.

Note: You may add cooked broccoli.

YIELD: 5 SERVINGS

Tomato Basil Soup

10 to 12 Roma tomatoes, peeled, or

1 (28-ounce) can whole tomatoes, drained

3 cups tomato juice

2 cups chicken stock

15 or more fresh basil leaves or dried basil

1 1/2 cups half-and-half

2 to 4 tablespoons unsalted butter, cut into pieces

1/2 teaspoon salt

1/2 teaspoon freshly ground pepper

Freshly grated Parmesan cheese

• Combine the tomatoes, tomato juice and stock in a large saucepan. Simmer for 30 minutes. Add the basil.

• Process in batches in a food processor or blender until smooth. Return to the saucepan over low heat. Whisk in the half-and-half, butter, salt and pepper.

• Cook over low heat for 30 minutes, whisking constantly. Ladle into soup bowls. Sprinkle with cheese.

YIELD: 6 TO 8 SERVINGS

Pasta e Fagioli

1 pound ground beef
1 small onion, chopped (1 cup)
1 carrot, julienned (1 cup)
3 ribs celery, chopped (1 cup)
2 garlic cloves, minced
2 (14-ounce) cans diced tomatoes
1 (15-ounce) can red kidney beans
1 (15-ounce) can Great Northern beans
1 (15-ounce) can tomato sauce
1 (12-ounce) can vegetable juice
    cocktail

1 tablespoon white vinegar
$1^1/2$ teaspoons salt
1 teaspoon oregano
1 teaspoon basil
$1/2$ teaspoon thyme
$1/2$ teaspoon pepper
6 to 8 cups ($1^1/2$ to 2 quarts) water
8 ounces ditali pasta or other
    small pasta

- Brown the ground beef in a large saucepan over medium heat; drain. Add the onion, carrot, celery and garlic. Sauté for 10 minutes. Add the tomatoes, undrained red kidney beans, undrained Great Northern beans, tomato sauce, vegetable juice cocktail, vinegar, salt, oregano, basil, thyme and pepper and mix well. Simmer for 1 hour.

- Bring the water to a boil over high heat in a large saucepan. Add the pasta. Cook for 10 minutes or until al dente; drain. Add to the soup.

- Simmer for 5 to 10 minutes. Ladle into soup bowls.

YIELD: 8 SERVINGS

Taco Soup

2 pounds ground beef

1 medium onion, chopped

1 (16-ounce) can kidney beans

1 (15-ounce) can hot chili beans

1 (4-ounce) can green chiles, drained

1 (11-ounce) can Mexicorn

1 (11-ounce) can Shoe Peg corn

3 (14-ounce) cans Mexican-style tomatoes

1 envelope taco seasoning mix

1 envelope ranch salad dressing mix

- Brown the ground beef and onion in a large skillet, stirring until the ground beef is crumbly; drain. Add the kidney beans, chili beans, green chiles, Mexicorn, Shoe Peg corn, tomatoes, taco seasoning mix and ranch salad dressing mix and mix well.

- Bring to a boil and reduce the heat. Simmer for 30 to 45 minutes.

YIELD: 8 SERVINGS

Grilled Chicken Chowder

1 cup chopped celery

$1/2$ cup chopped carrots

$1/2$ cup chopped red bell pepper

1 (15-ounce) can hominy

3 (14-ounce) cans chicken broth

3 chicken breasts, grilled and shredded

Chopped fresh cilantro to taste

3 cups (12 ounces) shredded Monterey Jack cheese

Chopped avocados to taste

Green onions to taste

Crisp tortilla strips to taste

- Cook the celery, carrots, bell pepper and hominy in the broth in a large saucepan until tender. Add the chicken, cilantro and cheese. Heat until the cheese melts, stirring constantly. Do not boil.

- Ladle into soup bowls. Top with chopped avocados, green onions and tortilla strips.

YIELD: 6 SERVINGS

Acapulco Gold Chicken Soup

1 pound boneless skinless chicken breasts
Garlic salt and pepper to taste
3 garlic cloves, minced
1 medium or large onion, chopped
1 green bell pepper, chopped
1/2 jalapeño chile, minced
2 (4-ounce) cans green chiles
1 (14- to 16-ounce) can whole kernel corn
4 cups hot water or chicken broth
16 ounces light Velveeta cheese, shredded
2 tablespoons cornstarch

- Season the chicken with garlic salt and pepper. Sauté in a nonstick skillet sprayed with nonstick cooking spray until cooked through. Remove from the heat. Cut into bite-size pieces.

- Sauté the garlic, onion, bell pepper and jalapeño chile in a Dutch oven sprayed with nonstick cooking spray until the vegetables are soft and the onion is translucent. Add the green chiles and corn. Add the chicken pieces and water. Stir in the cheese.

- Cook until the cheese melts, stirring constantly. Do not boil. Stir in the cornstarch. Simmer for 10 to 15 minutes or until thickened, stirring constantly. Ladle into soup bowls.

YIELD: 4 TO 6 SERVINGS

Chicken Vegetable Soup

3 (14-ounce) cans chicken broth

3 (12-ounce) cans tomato juice

2 cups chopped cooked chicken

1 (12-ounce) can whole kernel corn, drained

1 (15-ounce) package frozen lima beans, thawed

2 small red potatoes, peeled and chopped

1 medium onion, chopped

3/4 cup finely chopped celery

3/4 cup finely chopped carrots

4 1/2 teaspoons Worcestershire sauce

3/4 teaspoon garlic salt

1/2 teaspoon pepper

- Combine the broth, tomato juice, chicken, corn, lima beans, potatoes, onion, celery, carrots, Worcestershire sauce, garlic salt and pepper in a large stockpot.

- Bring to a boil. Cover and reduce the heat. Simmer for 1 hour, stirring occasionally. Ladle into soup bowls.

YIELD: 12 CUPS

White Chili

1 pound dried large white beans

6 cups chicken broth

2 garlic cloves, minced

2 medium onions, chopped

1 tablespoon vegetable oil

2 (4-ounce) cans chopped green chiles

2 teaspoons cumin

1^1/$_2$ teaspoons oregano

^{1}/$_4$ teaspoon cayenne pepper

4 cups chopped cooked chicken

1 tablespoon chopped fresh cilantro

3 cups (24 ounces) shredded Monterey Jack cheese

- Sort and rinse the beans. Combine the beans, broth, garlic and ^{1}/$_2$ of the onions in a large stockpot. Bring to a boil and reduce the heat. Simmer for 3 hours or until the beans are very soft, adding additional broth if needed.

- Sauté the remaining onions in the oil in a skillet until tender. Add the green chiles, cumin, oregano and cayenne pepper and mix thoroughly. Add to the bean mixture. Stir in the chicken.

- Simmer for 1 hour. Remove from the heat. Stir in the cilantro. Ladle into soup bowls. Sprinkle with the cheese.

YIELD: 8 TO 10 SERVINGS

Artichoke Oyster Soup

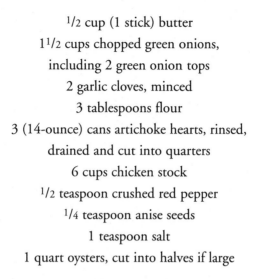

1/2 cup (1 stick) butter

1 1/2 cups chopped green onions,

including 2 green onion tops

2 garlic cloves, minced

3 tablespoons flour

3 (14-ounce) cans artichoke hearts, rinsed,

drained and cut into quarters

6 cups chicken stock

1/2 teaspoon crushed red pepper

1/4 teaspoon anise seeds

1 teaspoon salt

1 quart oysters, cut into halves if large

- Melt the butter in a large heavy stockpot. Add the green onions and garlic. Sauté for 3 to 5 minutes or until tender. Add the flour.

- Cook for 5 minutes, stirring constantly. Stir in the artichoke hearts. Add the stock, red pepper, anise seeds and salt.

- Cook for 20 minutes. Add the undrained oysters. Simmer for 10 minutes. Do not boil or overcook. Ladle into soup bowls.

Note: This soup is most delicious if made the day before serving, allowing the flavors to blend. If you want to drink the soup from mugs, purée in a blender and serve garnished with a lemon slice.

Yield: 12 to 14 servings

Roasted Pepper Shrimp Bisque

5 large red bell peppers

3 1/2 cups chicken stock or canned reduced-sodium chicken broth

1 teaspoon paprika

1 teaspoon sugar

3/4 cup whipping cream

1/2 cup grated Romano cheese

Hot pepper sauce to taste

Salt and pepper to taste

1 tablespoon olive oil

16 large uncooked shrimp, peeled, deveined and coarsely chopped

- Arrange the bell peppers on a baking sheet. Bake at 450 degrees for 3 minutes or until dark and blistered. Enclose in a paper bag. Let stand for 10 minutes. Peel the bell peppers and remove the seeds. Julienne 1 of the bell peppers. Chop the remaining bell peppers coarsely.

- Combine the chopped bell peppers and stock in a large heavy saucepan. Bring to a boil and reduce the heat. Simmer for 5 minutes or until the bell peppers are tender. Purée the mixture in batches in a blender or food processor until smooth. Return to the saucepan. Stir in the paprika and sugar. Simmer for 5 minutes to blend the flavors. (You may prepare up to 1 day ahead up to this point. Store the soup and julienned bell peppers separately in the refrigerator.)

- Whisk in the cream and cheese. Season with hot pepper sauce, salt and pepper. Heat the olive oil in a medium skillet over medium-high heat. Add the reserved bell pepper strips and shrimp. Sauté for 3 minutes or until the shrimp turn pink. Season with salt and pepper.

- Reheat the soup if needed. Divide the shrimp mixture into 4 soup bowls. Ladle the soup around the shrimp mixture. Garnish with fresh basil.

YIELD: 4 SERVINGS

Shrimp and Black Bean Chili

1 onion, chopped

1 tablespoon vegetable oil

1 small green bell pepper, chopped

1 small yellow bell pepper, chopped

1 small red bell pepper, chopped

1 cup chicken broth

1 (28-ounce) can whole tomatoes, chopped

2 (16-ounce) cans black beans, drained and rinsed

$1/2$ cup picante sauce

$1^{1}/2$ teaspoons cumin

$1/2$ teaspoon basil

$1/2$ teaspoon cayenne pepper

$1/2$ teaspoon garlic powder

$1^{1}/2$ teaspoons salt

2 pounds medium uncooked shrimp, peeled

- Sauté the onion in the oil in a skillet until translucent. Add the bell peppers. Cook until tender. Add the broth, undrained tomatoes, black beans, picante sauce, cumin, basil, cayenne pepper, garlic powder and salt and mix well.

- Cook for 20 to 25 minutes. Add the shrimp. Cook until the shrimp turn pink. Serve immediately over hot cooked rice.

YIELD: 8 SERVINGS

Per Serving (excluding unknown items): 280 Calories; 5 g Fat (17.0% calories from fat); 31 g Protein; 25 g Carbohydrate; 173 mg Cholesterol; 1141 mg Sodium. Exchanges: 1 Grain (Starch); $3^{1}/2$ Lean Meat; $1^{1}/2$ Vegetable; $1/2$ Fat.

Herbed Shrimp Soup

1 tablespoon olive oil
1 medium white onion, thinly sliced
1 pound ripe tomatoes, chopped
1 to 3 jalapeño chiles, seeded and minced
3 cups bottled clam juice
3 cups unsalted fat-free chicken broth
1 teaspoon oregano
1 pound medium shrimp, shelled and deveined
1 lime, cut into wedges

- Heat the olive oil in a large saucepan over medium heat. Add the onion. Sauté for 3 minutes or until softened. Add the tomatoes and jalapeño chiles. Cook for 3 minutes. Add the clam juice, broth and oregano.

- Bring to a boil and reduce the heat. Simmer for 5 minutes. Add the shrimp. Simmer for 5 minutes or until the shrimp turn pink.

- To serve, divide the shrimp evenly among 6 soup bowls. Spoon the broth and vegetables over the top. Squeeze lime wedges over each serving.

YIELD: 6 SERVINGS

Corn and Seafood Chowder

1 onion, chopped

1/2 cup (1 stick) butter

1/4 cup flour

2 (10-ounce) packages frozen whole kernel corn, or

4 cups frozen whole kernel corn

2 cups chicken broth

1 medium potato, chopped

1 carrot, shredded

2 cups heavy cream

3 cups milk

1 tablespoon lemon juice

3 dashes of Tabasco sauce

Salt and pepper to taste

1 1/2 pounds seafood

2 slices bacon, crisp-cooked and crumbled

- Sauté the onion in the butter in a stockpot. Add the flour. Cook until blended, stirring constantly. Add the corn, broth, potato and carrot.

- Cook for 10 minutes or until the potato is tender. Add the cream, milk and lemon juice. Bring to a gentle boil and reduce the heat. Season with the Tabasco sauce, salt and pepper. Stir in the seafood.

- Simmer until thickened and heated through. Ladle into soup bowls. Sprinkle with crumbled bacon.

Note: For the seafood, you may use crabmeat, shrimp, crawfish or a combination of all three.

YIELD: 10 TO 12 SERVINGS

Hot Ham Sandwiches

1 (8-ounce) container soft margarine
2 tablespoons Reese's Bavarian wine mustard
1 tablespoon prepared mustard
1/2 (2-ounce) container poppy seeds
12 onion buns, split
24 slices Swiss cheese
8 ounces precooked shaved ham

- Combine the margarine, wine mustard, prepared mustard and poppy seeds in a bowl and mix well. Spread generously on the split side of the buns.

- Layer 1 slice cheese, ham and 1 slice cheese on the bottom half of each bun. Replace the tops. Wrap each sandwich in heavy-duty foil.

- Bake at 325 degrees for 20 to 30 minutes or until heated through.

Note: You may freeze the sandwiches before baking.

YIELD: 12 SERVINGS

Shrimp Burgers

1 pound frozen cooked shrimp

3 tablespoons chopped celery

2 tablespoons chopped scallions

2 tablespoons chopped fresh parsley

1 1/2 teaspoons lemon zest

3 tablespoons mayonnaise

1 cup corn bread crumbs or bread crumbs

1 egg, beaten

Salt and white pepper to taste

Tabasco sauce to taste

1 tablespoon peanut oil

- Thaw the shrimp. Remove the tails and pat dry. Chop the shrimp. Combine the shrimp, celery, scallions, parsley and lemon zest in a large bowl. Add the mayonnaise, corn bread crumbs and egg and whisk until evenly distributed. Season with salt, white pepper and Tabasco sauce. Shape into patties.

- Brown 2 patties at a time in the peanut oil in a skillet. Drain on paper towels. Serve on hamburger buns with lettuce, tomato and tartar sauce.

YIELD: 4 SERVINGS

The Original Waldorf Salad

1 cup walnut halves

1/2 cup mayonnaise

1/4 cup plain yogurt

1 teaspoon prepared mustard

Pinch of dry mustard

Juice of 1/2 lemon

4 to 6 tart apples, peeled and chopped (2 cups)

1 to 2 cups finely chopped inner celery ribs (white part only)

Salt and freshly ground pepper to taste

2 bunches tender greens, such as arugula, baby kale or

pepper cress, rinsed and dried

2 tablespoons olive oil

1 tablespoon fresh lemon juice

- Spread the walnut halves on a baking sheet. Bake at 325 degrees for 4 to 5 minutes or until aromatic and lightly toasted. Remove from the oven to cool.

- Combine the mayonnaise, yogurt, prepared mustard, dry mustard and juice of 1/2 lemon in a large bowl. Fold in the apples and celery. Season with salt and pepper.

- Toss the salad greens in a large bowl. Add the olive oil, 1 tablespoon lemon juice, salt and pepper and toss well. Divide evenly among 4 salad plates. Spoon the apple mixture on the prepared plates. Sprinkle with the toasted walnuts. Garnish with celery leaves.

YIELD: 4 SERVINGS

Light Waldorf Salad

1 Granny Smith apple, cored and chopped
1 Red Delicious apple, cored and chopped
1 cup sliced red seedless grapes
1/2 cup chopped celery
1/2 cup macadamia nuts, chopped
1 cup reduced-fat vanilla yogurt
Juice of 1 orange
Ground cinnamon to taste

• Combine the Granny Smith apple, Red Delicious apple, grapes, celery and nuts in a large bowl and toss to mix. Blend the yogurt and orange juice in a bowl. Pour over the apple mixture and toss to coat. Sprinkle with cinnamon before serving.

Note: This is light and delicious. For variation, add 1/2 cup marshmallows.

YIELD: 8 SERVINGS

Per Serving (excluding unknown items): 122 Calories; 7 g Fat (45.8% calories from fat); 3 g Protein; 15 g Carbohydrate; 1 mg Cholesterol; 26 mg Sodium. Exchanges: 0 Grain (Starch); 0 Lean Meat; 0 Vegetable; 1/2 Fruit; 1 Fat; 1/2 Other Carbohydrates.

Cranberry Salad

1 (16-ounce) can whole cranberry sauce
1 (15-ounce) can crushed pineapple, drained
3 bananas, mashed
1 cup pecans, chopped
9 ounces whipped topping

• Combine the cranberry sauce, pineapple, bananas and pecans in a large bowl and mix well. Fold in the whipped topping. Spoon into cupcake cups. Freeze until firm.

YIELD: 20 SERVINGS

Fruited Cobb Salad with Poppy Seed Dressing

1/2 head iceberg lettuce

1/2 head romaine

1 head Belgian endive

1 orange, sectioned and chopped

1/2 fresh pineapple, chopped

10 strawberries, thinly sliced

1/2 honeydew melon, seeded and chopped

1/2 cantaloupe, seeded and chopped

Poppy Seed Dressing (below)

1/4 bunch fresh watercress, trimmed

1/4 head radicchio, trimmed

- Rinse the iceberg lettuce, romaine and Belgian endive and pat dry. Tear into a large salad bowl. Add the orange, pineapple, strawberries, honeydew melon and cantaloupe. Pour Poppy Seed Dressing over the top and toss to coat.

- Garnish with watercress and radicchio.

Note: This makes a beautiful presentation. It is great to serve in the summer with all of the fresh fruits.

YIELD: 12 SERVINGS

Poppy Seed Dressing

Also great served with avocados and grapefruit.

3/4 cup sugar

1 teaspoon dry mustard

1 teaspoon salt

1/3 cup white vinegar

1 1/2 tablespoons onion juice

1 cup vegetable oil

1 1/2 tablespoons poppy seeds

- Mix the sugar, dry mustard, salt and vinegar in a bowl. Stir in the onion juice. Add the oil in a fine stream, beating constantly until thick. Stir in the poppy seeds. Store in the refrigerator until ready to serve.

Note: To obtain the onion juice from an onion, cut the onion into halves and scrape with a knife or grater.

Orange Salad

1 (6-ounce) package orange gelatin
1 cup boiling water
1 pint orange sherbet (2 cups)
8 ounces whipped topping
1 (11-ounce) can mandarin oranges, drained

• Dissolve the gelatin in the boiling water in a large bowl. Add the orange sherbet and stir until smooth. Fold in the whipped topping and mandarin oranges.

• Pour into individual salad molds or a 9×13-inch dish. Chill until set.

YIELD: 10 TO 12 SERVINGS

Apricot Nectar Pear Salad

1 (12-ounce) can apricot nectar
1/4 cup pear juice
1 (6-ounce) package orange gelatin
1 teaspoon lemon juice
3 ounces cream cheese, softened
1/3 cup nuts, finely chopped
8 canned pear halves

• Bring the apricot nectar and pear juice to a boil in a small saucepan. Pour over the gelatin in a bowl and stir until the gelatin is dissolved. Stir in the lemon juice.

• Mix the cream cheese and nuts in a bowl. Shape into 8 balls. Place a ball in the center of each pear half. Invert into individual salad molds. Pour the gelatin mixture over the pears.

• Chill until set. Serve on lettuce leaves.

YIELD: 8 SERVINGS

Tossed Strawberry Salad

1 cup olive oil

1/2 cup red wine vinegar

2 garlic cloves

1/2 teaspoon paprika

1/2 teaspoon salt

1/2 teaspoon white pepper

1 head red leaf lettuce

1 head iceberg lettuce

1 pint strawberries, sliced

1/2 cup walnut halves

1 cup (4 ounces) shredded Monterey Jack cheese

- Blend the olive oil, vinegar, garlic, paprika, salt and white pepper in a bowl.

- Combine the red leaf lettuce, iceberg lettuce, strawberries, walnuts and cheese in a salad bowl and toss to mix. Pour the dressing over the salad when ready to serve and toss to coat.

YIELD: 8 TO 10 SERVINGS

Greens Salad with Warm Pecan Dressing

3 cups shredded fresh mustard greens

3 cups shredded fresh turnip greens

2 tablespoons fresh lemon juice

1/4 cup honey

2 tablespoons Dijon mustard

1/4 cup pecans, coarsely chopped

1/4 cup vegetable oil

- Toss the mustard greens and turnip greens in a large bowl.

- Combine the lemon juice, honey and Dijon mustard in a small bowl and mix well. Cook the honey mixture and pecans in the hot oil in a small skillet over medium heat for 2 minutes, stirring frequently.

- Pour over the greens and serve immediately.

Note: When using mustard and turnip greens, make sure to pick young greens to avoid bitterness. Mixed salad greens may be substituted.

YIELD: 6 SERVINGS

Per Servings (excluding unknown items): 173 Calories; 12 g Fat (61.0% calories from fat); 2 g Protein; 16 g Carbohydrate; 0 mg Cholesterol; 81 mg Sodium. Exchanges: 0 Grain (Starch); 0 Lean Meat; 1/2 Vegetable; 0 Fruit; 2 1/2 Fat; 1 Other Carbohydrates.

Vintner's Salad

4 heads Bibb lettuce, torn

2 heads romaine, torn

1 cup walnut halves

1 cup (4 ounces) shredded Gruyère cheese or Muenster cheese

1 cup olive oil

1/4 cup red wine, such as burgundy

2 tablespoons plus 2 teaspoons red wine vinegar

2 tablespoons Dijon mustard

2 teaspoons salt

1 1/2 teaspoons pepper

• Combine the Bibb lettuce, romaine, walnut halves and cheese in a salad bowl and toss to mix.

• Combine the olive oil, red wine, vinegar, Dijon mustard, salt and pepper in an airtight container and shake well. Pour over the lettuce mixture and toss to coat.

YIELD: 16 SERVINGS

Spinach Salad with Chutney Dressing

1 large or 2 small bunches spinach
6 to 8 mushrooms, sliced
1 (8-ounce) can sliced water chestnuts, drained
6 to 10 slices bacon, crisp-cooked and crumbled
1/2 cup (2 ounces) shredded Gruyère cheese
1/4 cup thinly sliced red onion
Chutney Dressing (below)

• Combine the spinach, mushrooms, water chestnuts, bacon, cheese and red onion in a salad bowl and toss to mix.

• Pour Chutney Dressing over the salad just before serving and toss to coat.

Yield: 4 to 6 servings

Chutney Dressing

1/4 cup red wine vinegar
1/4 cup undrained finely chopped chutney
1 garlic clove, minced
2 tablespoons Dijon mustard
2 tablespoons sugar

• Combine the vinegar, chutney, garlic, Dijon mustard and sugar in a bowl and mix well.

Crunchy Coleslaw

1/2 cup vegetable oil

1/3 cup apple vinegar

1/2 cup sugar

2 tablespoons soy sauce

1/2 teaspoon salt

1/4 teaspoon pepper

2 (3-ounce) packages chicken ramen noodles

2 small packages coleslaw

1 bunch green onions, chopped

1 small package slivered almonds

1 small package sunflower seeds

- Combine the oil, vinegar, sugar, soy sauce, salt, pepper and seasoning packet from the ramen noodles in a bowl and mix well.

- Combine the coleslaw and green onions in a large bowl and toss to mix. Add the dressing and toss to coat. Crumble the ramen noodles over the top just before serving. Sprinkle with the almonds and sunflower seeds.

Note: You may add cooked chicken breasts to serve as an entrée.

YIELD: 6 TO 8 SERVINGS

Corn Bread Salad

2 packages corn bread mix
1 cup chopped celery
1 cup chopped bell peppers
1 cup chopped green onions
2 tomatoes, chopped
1 (16-ounce) can whole kernel corn, drained
1 cup mayonnaise

• Prepare and bake the corn bread mix using the package directions. Remove from the oven to cool. Crumble the corn bread into a large bowl. Add the celery, bell peppers, green onions, tomatoes and corn and mix well. Stir in the mayonnaise.

Note: Best made 1 day in advance to allow the flavors to blend.

YIELD: 8 TO 10 SERVINGS

Sour Cream Potato Salad

1 cup sour cream
3 green onions, thinly sliced
2 tablespoons parsley
1/2 teaspoon salt
2 teaspoons prepared horseradish
1 1/2 cups mayonnaise
8 medium potatoes, boiled and sliced

• Mix the sour cream, green onions, parsley, salt, horseradish and mayonnaise in a bowl. Alternate layers of the potatoes and sour cream mixture in a shallow dish. Chill, covered, for 12 hours or longer before serving.

SERVES 8 TO 10

Layered Vegetable Salad with Caper and Thyme Dressing

4 cups thinly sliced red onions (about 3 medium)

2 (10-ounce) packages frozen peas

Salt to taste

8 cups thinly sliced napa cabbage (about 1 1/2 pounds)

3 cups chopped yellow bell peppers (about 3 large)

3/4 cup plain yogurt

3/4 cup mayonnaise

2 tablespoons drained capers, minced

1 1/2 teaspoons fresh thyme leaves, minced

Pepper to taste

- Soak the red onions in cold water to cover in a bowl for 10 minutes. Drain and pat dry.

- Cook the peas in boiling salted water to cover in a saucepan for 1 minute. Drain and pat dry.

- Layer the cabbage, red onions, bell peppers and peas in a large deep glass bowl.

- Whisk the yogurt, mayonnaise, capers, thyme, salt and pepper to taste in a bowl. Spread evenly over the peas. Chill, covered, for 6 to 24 hours.

- Toss the salad and season with salt and pepper just before serving.

YIELD: 16 SERVINGS

Marinated Vegetable Salad

1 (11-ounce) can white Shoe Peg corn, drained
1 (14-ounce) can French-style green beans, drained
1 (15-ounce) can petite green peas, drained
1 cup chopped onion
1 cup chopped celery
1 green bell pepper, chopped
1 red bell pepper, chopped
$1/2$ teaspoon salt
$1/2$ teaspoon pepper
1 cup sugar
$1/2$ cup vinegar
$1/2$ cup vegetable oil

- Combine the corn, green beans, peas, onion, celery, bell peppers, salt and pepper in a large bowl and mix well.

- Heat the sugar, vinegar and oil in a small saucepan until the sugar dissolves, stirring frequently. Pour over the vegetables.

- Chill, covered, until ready to serve.

YIELD: 8 TO 10 SERVINGS

Panzanella (Tuscan Bread Salad)

Arkansas summers scream tomatoes. Here's a great recipe perfect for picnics and cookouts that takes advantage of summer's bounty—and that nuisance leftover bread. If you like great bread, get it from Scotty McGehee in Little Rock (odds are you won't have leftovers, so buy extra—it's worth it).

1 pound ripe tomatoes	20 large basil leaves, chopped
1 pound dry Italian or French bread, cut into pieces	1 small bunch parsley, chopped
	1/2 cup olive oil
2 cucumbers, peeled, seeded and chopped	1/4 cup red wine vinegar
	Red chili flakes to taste
1 red onion, sliced	Salt and pepper to taste
3 ribs celery, chopped	

• Cut the tomatoes into quarters. Remove the seeds and chop the tomatoes, reserving the juice. Combine the bread, chopped tomatoes, reserved tomato juice, cucumbers, onion, celery, basil and parsley in a large bowl and toss to mix well. Whisk the olive oil and vinegar in a bowl. Pour over the bread mixture and toss to mix well. Season with red chili flakes, salt and pepper. Chill, covered, for 15 minutes before serving.

YIELD: 8 TO 10 SERVINGS

Janie's Chicken Salad

2 cups chopped cooked chicken breasts	1/4 teaspoon celery salt
1 cup finely chopped celery	1/2 teaspoon cayenne pepper
1 cup Hellmann's mayonnaise	1 teaspoon MSG (optional)
Juice of 1 lemon	Salt to taste

• Combine the chicken, celery, mayonnaise, lemon juice, celery salt, cayenne pepper, MSG and salt in a bowl and mix well. Chill, covered, until ready to serve.

Note: This delicious salad also makes a wonderful sandwich filling.

YIELD: 4 SERVINGS

Wild Rice Chicken Salad

2 (6-ounce) packages long grain and wild rice mix

2 (6-ounce) jars marinated artichoke hearts

4 cups chopped cooked chicken

1 medium red bell pepper, chopped

2 ribs celery, thinly sliced

5 green onions, chopped

1 (2-ounce) can sliced black olives, drained

1 cup mayonnaise

1$^1/_2$ teaspoons curry powder

- Cook the rice using the package directions.

- Drain the artichoke hearts, reserving $^1/_2$ cup of the marinade. Combine the rice, artichoke hearts, chicken, bell pepper, celery, green onions and olives in a large bowl and toss to mix well.

- Mix the mayonnaise, curry powder and reserved liquid in a small bowl. Pour over the chicken mixture and toss to mix well.

- Chill, covered, for 8 hours. Serve on lettuce leaves.

YIELD: 8 SERVINGS

Creamy Parmesan and Garlic Dressing

2 teaspoons chopped garlic
1/4 cup extra-virgin olive oil
3 tablespoons red wine vinegar
1/2 cup grated Parmesan cheese
1/2 teaspoon freshly cracked black pepper, or to taste

- Whisk the garlic, olive oil, vinegar, cheese and pepper in a bowl until creamy. Adjust the seasonings to taste.

- Serve with your favorite salad mix.

SERVES 4

Raspberry Dressing

3/4 cup lime juice
3/4 cup seedless raspberry jam
3 tablespoons vegetable oil
3 garlic cloves, pressed
3/4 teaspoon salt
3/4 teaspoon ground red pepper

- Process the lime juice, raspberry jam, oil, garlic, salt and red pepper in a blender until smooth.

- Serve with your favorite salad mix.

YIELD: 6 SERVINGS

Per Serving (excluding unknown items): 168 Calories; 7 g Fat (34.5% calories from fat); 1 g Protein; 29 g Carbohydrate; 0 mg Cholesterol; 283 mg Sodium. Exchanges: 0 Grain (Starch); 0 Vegetable; 0 Fruit; 1 1/2 Fat; 1 1/2 Other Carbohydrates.

Brunch & Bread

Arkansas River
and Agriculture
in
Pine Bluff
1908

The Arkansas River Mural

Discover Pine Bluff

Pine Bluff is a hometown with the big-city feel. All can feel welcome in the city that gives you the Pine Bluff Symphony, the Arts and Science Center for Southeast Arkansas, an eighteen-hole public golf course at Harbor Oaks, and regular bass fishing tournaments at the Pine Bluff/Jefferson County Regional Park. Our standards are high and our hospitality is overflowing. Come and discover what you've been missing. Come and discover Pine Bluff.

SPONSOR

JUNIOR LEAGUE OF PINE BLUFF

Women building better communities

Spinach Gratin

4 cups (1 quart) milk	1/4 cup finely chopped onion
7 tablespoons butter or margarine	3 tablespoons butter or margarine
1 cup flour	2 tablespoons flour
8 eggs	1/2 cup half-and-half
1 teaspoon salt	2 (10-ounce) packages frozen chopped
1/4 teaspoon white pepper	spinach, thawed, drained and
1/4 teaspoon ground nutmeg	squeezed dry
2 cups (8 ounces) shredded	Salt and black pepper to taste
Swiss cheese	2/3 cup shredded Swiss cheese

- Bring the milk to a boil in a saucepan and remove from the heat. Melt 7 tablespoons butter in a large saucepan. Stir in 1 cup flour. Cook over low heat for 2 minutes or until frothy, stirring constantly. Remove from the heat. Whisk in the hot milk gradually.

- Bring to a boil over medium heat, whisking constantly. Remove from the heat. Add the eggs 1 at a time, mixing well after each addition. Season with 1 teaspoon salt, white pepper and nutmeg. (The sauce may be slightly lumpy.) Stir in 2 cups cheese. Place a piece of waxed paper directly on the sauce to prevent a skin from forming.

- Sauté the onion in 3 tablespoons butter in a medium skillet for 8 minutes or until soft and beginning to brown. Sprinkle with 2 tablespoons flour. Cook for 2 minutes, stirring constantly. Add the half-and-half. Bring to a boil over medium heat, stirring constantly. Stir in the spinach. Season with salt and black pepper to taste.

- Spread 1/2 of the cheese sauce in a greased 9×13-inch baking dish. Layer the spinach mixture and remaining cheese sauce in the prepared baking dish. Sprinkle with 2/3 cup cheese. Bake, uncovered, at 400 degrees for 25 to 30 minutes or until the top is golden brown and bubbly.

Note: For Broccoli Gratin, use two 10-ounce packages frozen chopped broccoli, cooked, drained and finely chopped instead of the spinach.

YIELD: 12 TO 16 SERVINGS

Florentine Chicken Ring

1 (10-ounce) can chunk white chicken, drained and flaked
1/2 cup finely chopped red bell pepper
1 (10-ounce) package frozen chopped spinach, thawed and drained
1 cup (4 ounces) shredded sharp Cheddar cheese
1/3 cup mayonnaise
1 teaspoon lemon zest
1/2 teaspoon salt
1/8 teaspoon ground nutmeg
2 (8-count) cans refrigerated crescent rolls

- Combine the chicken, bell pepper, spinach, cheese, mayonnaise, lemon zest, salt and nutmeg in a bowl and mix well.

- Unroll the crescent roll dough and separate into 16 triangles. Arrange in a circle on a 13-inch baking stone with the wide ends of the triangles overlapping in the center and the points toward the outside, leaving a 5-inch opening in the center.

- Scoop the chicken mixture evenly onto the widest end of each triangle. Bring the outside points of the triangles up over the filling and tuck under the wide ends of the dough at the center of the ring. The filling will not be completely covered.

- Bake at 375 degrees for 20 to 25 minutes or until golden brown. Cut into slices to serve.

Note: Makes a great brunch dish or a really "heavy" hors d'oeuvre for a cocktail party.

YIELD: 8 SERVINGS

Eggs Florentine

1 pound hot or mild bulk pork sausage

2 cups sliced fresh mushrooms

1/2 cup sliced green onions

2²/3 tablespoons margarine

12 eggs

2 cups (1 pint) whipping cream

1 cup (4 ounces) shredded Cheddar cheese

1 (10-ounce) package frozen chopped spinach, drained

1 cup (4 ounces) shredded Swiss cheese

Paprika to taste

- Brown the sausage in a skillet, stirring until crumbly; drain.

- Sauté the mushrooms and green onions in the margarine in a skillet until tender.

- Beat the eggs in a mixing bowl until frothy. Add the whipping cream and mix well.

- Sprinkle the Cheddar cheese in a lightly oiled 9×13-inch glass baking dish. Layer the spinach, sausage and mushroom mixture in the prepared dish. Pour the egg mixture over the layers. Sprinkle the Swiss cheese and paprika over the top.

- Bake at 350 degrees for 45 minutes or until set.

YIELD: 10 TO 12 SERVINGS

Overnight Ham and Cheese Bake

8 ounces mushrooms, sliced

1 tablespoon butter

6 slices bread

2 tablespoons butter

2 cups (8 ounces) shredded Cheddar cheese

12 ounces ham, thinly sliced

1 (7-ounce) can diced green chiles, drained

2 cups (8 ounces) shredded Monterey Jack cheese

6 eggs

2 cups milk

2 teaspoons salt

1/2 teaspoon paprika

1/2 teaspoon basil

1/4 teaspoon onion salt

1/2 teaspoon pepper

1/2 teaspoon dry mustard

- Sauté the mushrooms in 1 tablespoon butter in a skillet until tender. Spread the bread with 2 tablespoons butter. Arrange buttered side down in a 9×13-inch baking dish. Sprinkle with the Cheddar cheese. Layer the ham, sautéed mushrooms, green chiles and Monterey Jack cheese over the Cheddar cheese.

- Beat the eggs, milk, salt, paprika, basil, onion salt, pepper and dry mustard in a bowl. Pour over the layers. Chill, covered with plastic wrap, for 8 to 12 hours.

- Bake, uncovered, at 325 degrees for 50 minutes. Let stand for 10 minutes to set before serving.

Note: You may substitute 1 pound bulk pork sausage, crumbled, browned and drained, for the ham.

YIELD: 6 SERVINGS

Ham and Asparagus Cheesecake

1 sleeve round butter crackers, crushed

6 tablespoons butter or margarine, melted

8 ounces cream cheese, softened

3 eggs

1 cup sour cream

^{1}/4 cup flour

^{1}/4 teaspoon pepper

2 cups (8 ounces) shredded Swiss cheese

1^1/4 cups chopped cooked ham

2 (10-ounce) cans asparagus pieces, drained and chopped

4 green onions, minced

- Combine the crackers and butter in a bowl and mix well. Press into a 9-inch springform pan.

- Bake at 350 degrees for 10 minutes. Remove to a wire rack to cool. Reduce the oven temperature to 300 degrees.

- Beat the cream cheese at medium speed in a mixing bowl for 2 to 3 minutes or until light and fluffy. Add the eggs 1 at a time, mixing well after each addition. Add the sour cream, flour and pepper and mix well. Stir in the Swiss cheese.

- Pour ^{1}/3 of the cheese mixture into the prepared pan. Sprinkle evenly with the ham. Pour ^{1}/2 of the remaining cheese mixture over the ham. Sprinkle with the asparagus and green onions. Spread the remaining cheese mixture evenly over the top.

- Bake for 1 hour or until the center is set. Turn off the oven. Let stand in the oven for 1 hour with the oven door partially open.

- Chill, covered, if desired. Garnish with chopped green onions and/or asparagus tips.

Note: You may use 1 pound fresh asparagus, cut into 1-inch pieces and steamed until tender-crisp.

YIELD: 8 SERVINGS

Western Egg Casserole

5 (4-ounce) cans chopped green chiles, drained
1 (4-ounce) can chopped green jalapeño chiles, drained
6 cups (24 ounces) shredded Monterey Jack cheese
12 eggs, lightly beaten
1 (5-ounce) can reduced-fat evaporated milk
1 teaspoon pepper

- Sprinkle 1/2 of the green chiles and 1/2 of the jalapeño chiles in a buttered and floured 9×13-inch glass baking dish.

- Layer the cheese, the remaining green chiles and the remaining jalapeño chiles 1/2 at a time in the prepared dish.

- Beat the eggs, evaporated milk and pepper in a mixing bowl until smooth. Pour over the layers.

- Bake at 350 degrees for 35 minutes. Cool slightly. Cut into squares.

Note: You may use 6 cups shredded Monterey Jack/Colby cheese blend or 6 cups shredded Mexican four-cheese blend.

YIELD: 8 SERVINGS

Expired Eggs?
To determine if an egg is fresh, immerse it in a pan of cool, salted water. If the egg sinks, it is fresh. If it rises to the surface, throw it out.

Tarte à l'Oignon (Onion Pie)

1 refrigerated pie pastry

6 medium yellow onions, sliced

3 tablespoons butter

1/4 teaspoon salt

Freshly ground pepper to taste

Dash of ground nutmeg

3 egg yolks, lightly beaten

2/3 cup heavy cream

- Unfold the pie pastry and roll into a 10-inch circle. Fit the pastry into an 8-inch pie plate, fluting the edge.

- Sauté the onions in the butter in a skillet over medium heat. Simmer, covered, for 30 minutes, stirring occasionally. Season with salt, pepper and nutmeg.

- Beat the egg yolks and cream in a bowl. Stir into the onion mixture and remove from the heat. Pour into the prepared pie plate.

- Bake at 400 degrees for 30 minutes.

YIELD: 6 TO 8 SERVINGS

Asparagus and Cheese Quiche

1¹/2 pounds fresh asparagus

1 refrigerated pie pastry

¹/2 small onion, chopped

1 tablespoon butter

2 tablespoons Dijon mustard

2 cups (8-ounces) shredded Colby and Monterey Jack cheese

1¹/2 cups half-and-half

2 eggs

¹/4 teaspoon salt

¹/4 teaspoon pepper

- Snap off the tough ends of the asparagus, leaving about 5 inches. Cook in boiling water to cover in a saucepan for 30 seconds. Plunge immediately into ice water in a bowl to stop the cooking process. Reserve 9 of the asparagus spears. Chop the remaining spears coarsely.

- Unfold the pie pastry and roll into a 14-inch circle. Fit into a 10-inch deep-dish pie plate, fluting the edge. Line the pastry with foil and weight down with dried beans. Place on a baking sheet. Bake at 425 degrees for 10 minutes. Remove the beans and foil. Bake for 2 minutes longer. Reduce the oven temperature to 375 degrees.

- Sauté the onion in the butter in a skillet until tender. Brush the pastry with Dijon mustard. Layer ¹/2 of the cheese, chopped asparagus, onion and remaining cheese in the prepared pie plate. Arrange the reserved asparagus spears in the shape of a pin wheel over the top.

- Whisk the half-and-half, eggs, salt and pepper in a bowl. Pour evenly over the layers.

- Bake for 20 to 25 minutes or until set and golden brown.

YIELD: 6 TO 8 SERVINGS

Chicken Quiche

1 1/2 cups (6 ounces) shredded Swiss cheese
1 tablespoon flour
1 tablespoon chicken bouillon granules
2 cups chopped cooked chicken
1 cup milk
3 eggs, beaten
1 (4-ounce) jar chopped pimentos, drained
1 green bell pepper, chopped
1 tablespoon grated onion
1/2 teaspoon onion salt
Dash of white pepper
Dash of cayenne pepper
1 unbaked (9-inch) deep-dish pie shell

- Mix the cheese, flour, bouillon and chicken in a large bowl. Add the milk, eggs, pimentos, bell pepper, onion, onion salt, white pepper and cayenne pepper and mix well. Pour into the pie shell.

- Bake at 350 degrees for 40 to 45 minutes or until set. Let stand for 10 minutes before serving.

YIELD: 6 TO 8 SERVINGS

Ham Quiche

1 refrigerated pie pastry
8 ounces boiled ham, cut into small pieces
1 cup (4 ounces) shredded Swiss cheese
4 eggs
1 tablespoon flour
1 cup milk
1/2 cup heavy cream
1/4 teaspoon salt
Freshly ground pepper to taste

- Unroll the pie pastry and roll into a 10-inch circle. Fit into a 9-inch pie plate, trimming and fluting the edge. Layer the ham and cheese in the prepared pie plate.

- Combine the eggs, flour, milk, cream, salt and pepper in a bowl and mix well. Pour over the layers.

- Bake at 400 degrees for 30 to 45 minutes or until set. Cool for 5 to 10 minutes before serving.

Yield: 6 to 8 servings

Rosemary Cheese Strata

1 onion, chopped

2 tablespoons unsalted butter

1 (8-ounce) baguette

4 cups (16 ounces) shredded Monterey Jack cheese

1/4 cup minced fresh rosemary

3 cups whipping cream

10 eggs

1 teaspoon salt

Pepper to taste

- Sauté the onion in the butter in a skillet over medium heat until golden brown.

- Cut the baguette into 1-inch slices. Arrange on a baking sheet.

- Bake at 350 degrees until toasted.

- Layer the toasted baguette slices, cheese, sautéed onion and rosemary 1/2 at a time in a buttered 9×13-inch baking dish. Whisk the cream, eggs, salt and pepper in a bowl. Pour over the layers.

- Chill, covered, for 8 to 10 hours.

- Bake, uncovered, at 375 degrees for 40 minutes or until golden brown and bubbly.

YIELD: 10 SERVINGS

Italian Strata

1¹/2 pounds mild Italian sausage
1 pound zucchini, sliced
8 ounces fresh spinach, torn into
bite-size pieces
1 onion, thinly sliced
1 teaspoon dry mustard
1 teaspoon salt

¹/2 teaspoon freshly ground pepper
2 cups (8 ounces) shredded Cheddar
cheese
2 cups (8 ounces) shredded Swiss cheese
1¹/2 cups milk
7 eggs
10 slices white bread, torn

• Remove the casings and crumble the sausage into a skillet. Brown the sausage,
stirring until crumbly. Drain the sausage, reserving the drippings in the skillet. Sauté
the zucchini, spinach and onion in the reserved drippings in the skillet until tender.

• Combine the sausage, vegetable mixture, dry mustard, salt, pepper, Cheddar cheese,
Swiss cheese, milk, eggs and bread in a large bowl and mix well. Chill, covered, for
8 to 12 hours. Stir the sausage mixture and spoon into a greased 9×13-inch
baking dish.

• Bake at 325 degrees for 1¹/2 hours or until set, watching carefully during the last
30 minutes as the strata tends to brown quickly.

YIELD: 8 TO 12 SERVINGS

Cheese Grits

1 cup grits, cooked
¹/2 cup (1 stick) margarine
1 cup (4 ounces) shredded
American cheese

2 eggs, beaten
¹/2 cup milk

• Cook the grits using the package directions. Add the margarine and cheese. Heat
until melted, stirring constantly. Add the eggs and milk and mix well. Pour into a
baking dish. Bake at 350 degrees for 45 minutes.

YIELD: 8 SERVINGS

Blueberry Corn Pancakes

1 1/2 cups yellow cornmeal

1/4 cup whole wheat flour

1 teaspoon baking soda

1/2 teaspoon salt

2 tablespoons honey

2 tablespoons safflower oil

2 cups low-fat buttermilk

1 egg, lightly beaten

1 1/2 cups blueberries

- Mix the cornmeal, whole wheat flour, baking soda and salt in a medium bowl.

- Combine the honey, safflower oil, buttermilk and egg in a bowl and mix well. Stir in the cornmeal mixture. Let stand for 10 minutes to soften the cornmeal. Fold in the blueberries.

- Grease lightly a preheated skillet. Pour 1/4 cup batter into the skillet. Bake until bubbly. Turn and bake until golden brown. Repeat with the remaining batter.

SERVES 2

The Perfect Stack of Pancakes
When making pancakes try using a meat baster to distribute the perfect round pancake.

Baked French Toast with Berries

1 (8- or 9-ounce) loaf dry French bread

3 eggs

3 tablespoons sugar

1 teaspoon vanilla extract

2^1/4 cups milk

^{1}/2 cup flour

6 tablespoons dark brown sugar

^{1}/2 teaspoon cinnamon

^{1}/4 cup (^{1}/2 stick) butter or margarine

1 cup fresh or frozen blueberries

1 cup fresh or frozen strawberries

- Cut the bread diagonally into 1-inch slices. Arrange in a well-greased 9×13-inch baking dish.

- Beat the eggs, sugar and vanilla lightly in a medium bowl. Stir in the milk. Pour over the bread, turning the bread to coat well. Chill, covered, for 8 to 12 hours.

- Mix the flour, brown sugar and cinnamon in a small bowl. Cut in the butter until crumbly.

- Turn the bread in the baking dish. Layer the blueberries over the bread. Sprinkle evenly with the crumb mixture.

- Bake at 375 degrees for 40 minutes or until golden brown. Cut into squares. Top with the strawberries or serve on the side.

YIELD: 8 SERVINGS

Angel Biscuits

1 envelope dry yeast

$1/2$ cup lukewarm water

2 cups buttermilk

$3/4$ cup corn oil

5 cups self-rising flour

3 tablespoons sugar

- Dissolve the yeast in the lukewarm water in a large bowl. Add the buttermilk, corn oil, self-rising flour and sugar and mix well. Let rise in the refrigerator for 30 minutes.

- Pinch off enough dough for the desired number of biscuits. Shape into balls and slightly flatten. Arrange on an ungreased baking sheet.

- Bake at 425 degrees for 15 to 20 minutes or until brown.

Note: You may store the dough in the refrigerator for several days.

YIELD: 3 DOZEN

Garlic Spread

Prepare this easy spread while the biscuits are baking. Mix $1/2$ cup (1stick) melted butter, 1 teaspoon garlic powder, $1/4$ teaspoon salt, $1/8$ teaspoon onion powder and $1/8$ teaspoon parsley in a bowl. Brush over the hot biscuits.

Buttermilk Biscuits

2 cups flour
4 teaspoons baking powder
1/4 teaspoon baking soda
1/4 teaspoon salt
1/4 cup shortening or margarine
1 cup (about) buttermilk
Flour for dusting

- Sift the flour, baking powder, baking soda and salt into a bowl. Cut in the shortening until crumbly. Add enough of the buttermilk to form a nonsticky ball. Let rest for 30 minutes.

- Pat into a circle on a floured surface. Sprinkle a thin dusting of flour on top. Invert and roll 1/2 inch thick with a floured rolling pin. Cut with a biscuit cutter dipped in flour. Arrange 2 inches apart on an ungreased baking sheet.

- Bake at 400 degrees for 20 minutes or until golden brown on top.

Note: You may use a mixture of 1 cup milk and 1 tablespoon vinegar instead of the buttermilk.

YIELD: 10 TO 15 SERVINGS

Chocolate Gravy

Combine 3/4 cup sugar, 2 tablespoons baking cocoa, 2 tablespoons flour and 1/2 teaspoon salt in a saucepan. Whisk in enough of 2 cups milk to form a smooth paste. Cook over medium heat, stirring in the remaining milk gradually. Cook until thickened, stirring constantly. Stir in 2 tablespoons margarine and 1 teaspoon vanilla extract. Serve over hot buttered biscuits.

Sour Cream Coffee Cake

Pecan halves

1/2 cup chopped pecans

2 tablespoons sugar

1 tablespoon cinnamon

2 cups cake flour

1 teaspoon baking powder

1/8 teaspoon salt

1 cup (2 sticks) butter, softened

2 cups sugar

2 eggs

1 cup sour cream

1/2 teaspoon vanilla extract

- Coat a bundt pan generously with butter or shortening. Place a pecan half in each notch. Mix 1/2 cup chopped pecans, 2 tablespoons sugar and cinnamon in a small bowl. Sprinkle 2 tablespoons of the pecan mixture in the prepared pan.

- Sift the cake flour, baking powder and salt together. Cream the butter and 2 cups sugar in a mixing bowl until light and fluffy. Beat in the eggs. Add the sifted cake flour mixture gradually and mix well. Fold in the sour cream and vanilla.

- Layer the batter and remaining pecan mixture 1/3 at a time in the prepared pan, ending with the pecan mixture.

- Bake at 350 degrees for 55 to 60 minutes or until the cake pulls from the side of the pan. Cool in the pan for 10 minutes. Invert onto a wire rack to cool completely.

YIELD: 12 SERVINGS

Cream Cheese Braid

1 cup sour cream	4 cups flour
1/2 cup sugar	16 ounces cream cheese, softened
1 teaspoon salt	3/4 cup sugar
1/2 cup (1 stick) butter, melted	1 egg
2 envelopes dry yeast	1/8 teaspoon salt
1/2 cup warm water	2 teaspoons vanilla extract
2 eggs, beaten	Confectioners' Sugar Glaze (below)

• Heat the sour cream over low heat in a saucepan. Stir in 1/2 cup sugar, 1 teaspoon salt and butter. Cool to lukewarm. Dissolve the yeast in the warm water in a large bowl. Add the sour cream mixture, 2 eggs and the flour and mix well. Cover tightly and chill for 8 to 12 hours. Beat the cream cheese and 3/4 cup sugar in a mixing bowl until smooth. Add 1 egg, 1/8 teaspoon salt and the vanilla and mix well.

• Divide the dough into 4 equal portions. Roll each portion into an 8×12-inch rectangle on a well-floured surface. Spread 1/4 of the cream cheese mixture on each rectangle. Roll up beginning at the long side, pinching the ends and folding under slightly. Place seam side down on a greased baking sheet. Cut slits into each roll-up at 2-inch intervals about 2/3 of the way through the dough to resemble a braid. Cover and let rise for 1 hour or until doubled in bulk.

• Bake at 350 degrees for 20 minutes or until golden brown. Remove from the oven to cool slightly. Drizzle the warm braids with Confectioners' Sugar Glaze.

YIELD: 4 BRAIDS

Confectioners' Sugar Glaze

2 cups confectioners' sugar
1/4 cup milk
1 teaspoon vanilla extract

• Combine the confectioners' sugar, milk and vanilla in a bowl and mix well.

Hawaiian Banana Nut Bread

3 cups sifted flour

1 teaspoon baking soda

2 cups sugar

1 teaspoon cinnamon

1 teaspoon salt

2 eggs, beaten

3/4 cup vegetable oil

2 teaspoons vanilla extract

2 cups mashed bananas

1 (8-ounce) can crushed pineapple, drained

1 cup chopped nuts

- Mix the flour, baking soda, sugar, cinnamon and salt in a large bowl.

- Beat the eggs, oil, vanilla, bananas and pineapple in a mixing bowl. Add to the flour mixture and mix well. Stir in the nuts. Pour into 2 greased and floured 5×9-inch loaf pans.

- Bake at 350 degrees for 50 minutes. Cover the top of the loaves with foil. Bake for 20 minutes longer or until the loaves test done.

YIELD: 2 LOAVES

Buttermilk Chocolate Bread with Chocolate Honey Butter

1 1/2 cups flour

1/2 cup baking cocoa

1/2 teaspoon baking powder

1/2 teaspoon baking soda

1/2 teaspoon salt

1 cup (2 sticks) butter, softened

1 1/4 cups sugar

2 eggs

1 cup buttermilk

1/3 cup chopped pecans, macadamia nuts or walnuts

Chocolate Honey Butter (below)

- Mix the flour, baking cocoa, baking powder, baking soda and salt together. Cream the butter and sugar in a mixing bowl until light and fluffy. Add the eggs 1 at a time, beating well after each addition. Add the flour mixture and buttermilk alternately, mixing well after each addition. Fold in the pecans. Pour into a greased 5×9-inch loaf pan.

- Bake at 350 degrees for 1 hour or until a wooden pick inserted near the center comes out clean. Cool in the pan on a wire rack for 10 minutes. Invert onto the wire rack to cool completely. Cut into slices and serve with Chocolate Honey Butter.

YIELD: 1 LOAF

Chocolate Honey Butter

1/2 cup (1 stick) butter, softened

2 tablespoons honey

2 tablespoons chocolate syrup

- Beat the butter, honey and chocolate syrup in a small mixing bowl until smooth.

Lemon Bread

1¹/2 cups flour

1 teaspoon baking powder

3 tablespoons shortening

3 tablespoons butter, softened

1 cup sugar

Grated zest of 1 lemon

2 eggs

¹/2 cup milk

¹/2 cup chopped nuts

¹/4 cup sugar

Juice of 1 lemon

- Sift the flour and baking powder together. Cream the shortening, butter, 1 cup sugar and lemon zest in a mixing bowl until light and fluffy. Add the eggs and mix well. Add the flour mixture and milk alternately, mixing well after each addition. Fold in the nuts. Pour into a greased and floured 5×9-inch loaf pan.

- Bake at 350 degrees for 45 minutes or until the loaf tests done.

- Mix ¹/4 cup sugar and lemon juice in a small bowl. Pierce the hot bread with a fork. Pour the lemon mixture over the hot bread. Let stand for 5 minutes before removing from the pan.

YIELD: 1 LOAF

Strawberry Bread with Cream Cheese Spread

3 cups flour

2 cups sugar

1 teaspoon baking soda

1 teaspoon salt

1 teaspoon cinnamon

1/2 cup strawberry juice

2 (10-ounce) packages frozen strawberries, thawed

1 cup vegetable oil

4 eggs, beaten

8 ounces cream cheese, softened

1/2 cup strawberry juice

- Mix the flour, sugar, baking soda, salt and cinnamon in a large bowl and make a well in the center. Add 1/2 cup strawberry juice, strawberries, oil and eggs and mix well. Pour into 2 greased and floured 4×8-inch loaf pans.

- Bake at 350 degrees for 1 hour or until a wooden pick inserted in the center comes out clean.

- Beat the cream cheese with enough of the 1/2 cup strawberry juice to make a spreadable consistency. Spread over the loaves. Chill until ready to serve.

Note: These loaves freeze well.

YIELD: 2 LOAVES

Apple Muffins

3¹/2 cups flour

3 cups finely chopped peeled apples

2 cups sugar

1 teaspoon salt

1 teaspoon baking soda

1 teaspoon cinnamon

1¹/2 cups vegetable oil

1 teaspoon vanilla extract

- Combine the flour, apples, sugar, salt, baking soda and cinnamon in a large bowl and mix well. Stir in the oil and vanilla. (The consistency of the batter will vary with the type of apples used.) Pour into greased and floured muffin cups, filling 1/2 to 2/3 full.

- Bake at 350 degrees for 25 to 30 minutes or until the muffins test done.

YIELD: 2 DOZEN

The Crust Counts
For delicate, tender crusts on muffins, coffee cakes, and nut breads, use shiny pans and baking sheets that reflect the heat.

Blueberry Muffins

2 cups flour	2 eggs
1 teaspoon baking powder	1/2 cup buttermilk
1/2 teaspoon baking soda	1 teaspoon vanilla extract
1/2 teaspoon salt	1 teaspoon lemon extract
1/2 cup (1 stick) butter, melted	1 cup blueberries
1 cup sugar	

- Sift the flour, baking powder, baking soda and salt together. Whisk the butter, sugar, eggs, buttermilk, vanilla and lemon extract in the order listed in a large bowl. Whisk in the flour mixture until smooth. Fold in the blueberries. Fill greased and floured muffin cups 2/3 full.

- Bake at 375 degrees for 13 minutes until light brown on top.

YIELD: 1 DOZEN

Vanilla Muffins

1/2 cup (1 stick) butter, melted	1/4 cup baking powder
4 cups flour	2 eggs
2 cups sugar	1 tablespoon vanilla extract
2 cups milk	

- Combine the butter, flour, sugar, milk, baking powder, eggs and vanilla in a bowl an and mix well. Pour into greased muffin cups, filling 2/3 full.

- Bake at 400 degrees for 20 minutes.

YIELD: 2 1/2 DOZEN

Sour Cream Corn Muffins

1 cup self-rising yellow cornmeal mix

$1/2$ teaspoon salt

$1/4$ cup vegetable oil

1 (8-ounce) can cream-style corn

1 cup sour cream

2 eggs, lightly beaten

- Combine the cornmeal mix, salt, oil, corn, sour cream and eggs in a bowl and mix until smooth. Spoon into greased muffin cups, filling $2/3$ full.

- Bake at 400 degrees for 25 minutes or until golden brown. Remove from the pan and serve immediately.

YIELD: 1 DOZEN

Dynamiting the Arkansas River Levee

On December 8, 1908, after the appeal to the United States Army Corps of Engineers to breech the levee was denied, the local authorities took matters into their own hands and dispatched a crew by steam ferry to dynamite the levee. The explosion was successful and it saved the Courthouse, but the river took its toll further downstream.

Broccoli Corn Bread

1 (10-ounce) package frozen chopped broccoli, thawed
1 package corn bread mix
1/2 cup (1 stick) butter, melted
8 ounces (2 cups) shredded Cheddar cheese
3 eggs, beaten
1 onion, chopped
3 garlic cloves, chopped
1/2 teaspoon salt
1/2 teaspoon ground red pepper

• Combine the broccoli, corn bread mix, butter, cheese, eggs, onion, garlic, salt and red pepper in a bowl and mix well. Pour into a lightly greased 9×13-inch baking dish.

• Bake at 375 degrees for 25 to 30 minutes or until golden brown.

YIELD: 15 SERVINGS

Dilled Corn Bread

1 (8-ounce) package corn muffin mix
1 egg
1/3 cup milk
1/4 cup fresh dill weed, finely chopped, or
1 tablespoon dried dill weed

• Combine the muffin mix, egg, milk and dill weed in a bowl and stir to form a slightly lumpy batter. Pour into a greased 5×9-inch loaf pan or muffin cups.

• Bake at 400 degrees for 15 to 20 minutes or until golden brown.

YIELD: 1 LOAF

Old-Fashioned Corn Bread

1 teaspoon vegetable oil

1/4 cup flour

1/2 cup cornmeal

1 tablespoon baking powder

1 1/2 teaspoons sugar

1/2 teaspoon salt

1 egg, beaten

1/2 cup milk

- Heat the oil in an 8-inch cast-iron skillet in a 400-degree oven. Swirl the oil in the skillet until coated.

- Mix the flour, cornmeal, baking powder, sugar and salt in a bowl. Add the egg and milk and mix well to form a thick batter. Add the hot oil and mix well. Pour into the prepared skillet. (The batter should sizzle as it is poured into the hot skillet.)

- Bake for 18 to 20 minutes or until golden brown.

Note: You may substitute buttermilk for the milk and add 1/4 teaspoon baking soda.

YIELD: 8 TO 10 SERVINGS

*1927
Arkansas River
100-Year Flood*
In 1927, all of the Mississippi River Valley was flooded including Pine Bluff and Jefferson County. The United States Corps of Engineers called it a "100-year flood" because a flood of this magnitude only occurs once every 100 years. Levees broke on both sides of the Arkansas River, allowing enormous quantities of water to overwhelm the land and force families to abandon their property for refuge. The flood lasted from April 17, 1927 until the first of May.

Skillet Corn Bread

1 cup yellow cornmeal
1/2 cup flour
1 tablespoon baking powder
1/2 teaspoon salt
1 tablespoon sugar
1 cup buttermilk
1/4 cup bacon drippings
2 eggs, lightly beaten

• Grease a 9-inch cast-iron skillet. Heat in a 400-degree oven for 4 minutes.

• Mix the cornmeal, flour, baking powder, salt and sugar in a large bowl and make a well in the center. Combine the buttermilk, bacon drippings and eggs in a bowl and mix well. Add to the cornmeal mixture and stir just until moistened. Pour into the hot skillet.

• Bake at 400 degrees for 20 minutes or until golden brown. Remove from the skillet. Serve warm or at room temperature.

YIELD: 6 SERVINGS

Per Serving (excluding unknown items): 249 Calories; 11 g Fat (40.3% calories from fat); 6 g Protein; 31 g Carbohydrate; 73 mg Cholesterol; 531 mg Sodium. Exchanges: 1 1/2 Grain (Starch); 1/2 Lean Meat; 0 Non-Fat Milk; 2 Fat; 0 Other Carbohydrates.

Easy Homemade Bread

2 cups warm water
2 envelopes dry yeast
$1/4$ cup sugar
1 tablespoon salt
5 to 6 cups flour
2 tablespoons butter, melted

- Mix the water, yeast, sugar and salt in a large bowl. Let stand for 10 minutes or until bubbly. Add the flour and mix well. Let rise for $1^1/2$ hours or until doubled in bulk. Punch the dough down.

- Divide into 2 equal portions. Shape each portion into loaves. Place in 2 greased 5×8-inch loaf pans. Let rise for $1^1/2$ hours or until doubled in bulk.

- Bake at 350 degrees for 25 minutes or until golden brown. Brush with the melted butter.

YIELD: 2 LOAVES

Icebox Rolls

4 cups (1 quart) whole milk
1 cup sugar
1 cup shortening
2 envelopes dry yeast
3 cups sifted flour
1 tablespoon salt
1 teaspoon baking soda
4 cups sifted flour

- Heat the milk in a saucepan just to the boiling point. Add the sugar and shortening. Heat until the sugar dissolves, stirring constantly. Remove from the heat. Set the saucepan in a larger container of cold water and cool to lukewarm.

- Combine the lukewarm milk mixture, yeast and 3 cups flour in a large bowl and mix well. Let stand for 1 hour. Add the salt, baking soda and 4 cups flour and mix well. Place in a greased bowl, turning to coat the surface. Chill, covered, for 8 to 12 hours. (The dough will keep for several days in the refrigerator.)

- Spray muffin cups with nonstick cooking spray. Shape the dough into small round balls. Arrange 3 balls in each muffin cup. Cover with a kitchen towel. Let rise for several hours or until doubled in bulk.

- Bake at 400 degrees for 10 minutes.

YIELD: 3 1/2 DOZEN

Spinach and Cheese Bread

1 (10-ounce) package frozen chopped spinach,
thawed and squeezed dry
1 egg, beaten
2 tablespoons milk
1 tablespoon Dijon mustard
1 teaspoon garlic salt
1 cup (4 ounces) shredded mozzarella cheese
1 cup (4 ounces) shredded Cheddar cheese
1/3 cup grated Parmesan cheese
1/4 cup fresh white bread crumbs
1 (11-ounce) tube refrigerated Crusty French bread dough

- Mix the spinach, egg, milk, Dijon mustard and garlic salt in a medium bowl. Stir in the mozzarella cheese, Cheddar cheese, Parmesan cheese and bread crumbs.

- Unroll the dough on a lightly floured surface. Roll into a 13-inch square. Cut into halves forming two 6¹/₂×13-inch rectangles. Spoon ¹/₂ of the spinach mixture in a narrow strip lengthwise down the center of each rectangle, leaving ¹/₂-inch border on the short sides. Fold 1 long side of each rectangle over the spinach mixture; fold the remaining side over the top, enclosing the spinach mixture completely and overlapping the first side slightly. Seal the seam and short ends of each loaf.

- Arrange the loaves on a buttered large heavy baking sheet. Cut crosswise slits at 1-inch intervals in the top of each loaf.

- Bake at 375 degrees for 25 minutes or until golden brown. Loosen the loaves from the baking sheet with a metal spatula. Remove to wire racks. Cool for 15 minutes. Serve warm or at room temperature.

YIELD: 2 LOAVES

Tootie Bread

1 loaf French bread

8 slices Swiss cheese

1/2 cup (1 stick) margarine, softened

1/4 cup finely chopped onion

1 tablespoon prepared mustard

1 tablespoon poppy seeds

4 slices bacon, crisp-cooked and crumbled

- Cut the bread into 16 slices to but not through the bottom. Cut the cheese slices diagonally into halves. Place the cheese between the slices of bread. Place the bread loaf on a sheet of foil.

- Mix the margarine, onion, mustard and poppy seeds in a bowl. Spread over the top and side of the loaf. Sprinkle with the bacon. Wrap in the foil. Place on a baking sheet.

- Bake at 400 degrees for 20 minutes. Serve hot.

YIELD: 8 TO 10 SERVINGS

Vegetables & Side Dishes

Jefferson County Courthouse

When it comes to trust,

honesty and friendship,

some things should never change.

And for 100 years,

we have made sure they

remain the same.

SPONSOR

Creamed Artichokes and Onions

1 (16-ounce) bag white boiler onions

Salt to taste

2 (14-ounce) cans water-packed artichokes

1 green onion

1/2 cup (1 stick) butter

3/4 cup flour

Milk

1/2 teaspoon Worcestershire sauce

Paprika to taste

Red pepper and black pepper to taste

1 to 2 cups (4 to 8 ounces) shredded Monterey Jack cheese,

Cheddar cheese or your favorite blend

Bread crumbs

- Boil the onions in salted water in a saucepan until almost tender; drain. Place in a greased baking dish. Drain the artichokes, reserving the liquid. Layer the artichokes over the onions.

- Sauté the green onion in the butter in a skillet until tender. Add the flour, reserved artichoke liquid and enough milk to make a medium-thick sauce. Cook until thickened, stirring constantly. Stir in the Worcestershire sauce, paprika, red pepper and black pepper. Add the cheese. Heat until melted, stirring constantly. Pour over the layers. Top with the bread crumbs.

- Bake at 325 degrees for 45 minutes.

YIELD: 8 TO 10 SERVINGS

Sesame Asparagus

2¹/2 pounds asparagus

1/4 cup (1/2 stick) butter

2 tablespoons lemon juice

2 teaspoons sesame oil

2 tablespoons sesame seeds

1/4 teaspoon each salt and pepper

• Cook the asparagus in enough water to cover in a saucepan for 4 to 6 minutes. Drain and rinse in cold water. (You may make ahead and store in the refrigerator for up to 4 hours at this point.) Melt the butter in a skillet. Stir in the lemon juice, sesame oil, sesame seeds, salt and pepper. Add the asparagus. Cook until heated through.

Note: This was served at Charity Ball 1997.

YIELD: 8 TO 10 SERVINGS

Sweet-and-Sour Asparagus with Toasted Pecans

2 pounds fresh asparagus, trimmed

1/4 cup white vinegar

1/4 cup soy sauce

1/4 cup sugar

2 tablespoons vegetable oil

1/4 cup pecans, toasted and finely chopped

• Steam the asparagus for 6 to 8 minutes or until tender-crisp. Drain and rinse in cold water. Arrange the asparagus in a 9×13-inch baking dish. Combine the vinegar, soy sauce, sugar and oil in a bowl and mix well. Pour over the asparagus. Marinate, covered, in the refrigerator for 8 hours or longer.

• To serve, drain the asparagus, discarding the marinade. Arrange the asparagus on individual lettuce-lined serving plates. Sprinkle with the toasted pecans.

Note: You may microwave the asparagus in 2 tablespoons water for 5 to 7 minutes.

YIELD: 8 SERVINGS

Per Serving (excluding unknown items): 109 Calories; 6 g Fat (44.6% calories from fat); 3 g Protein; 13 g Carbohydrate; 0 mg Cholesterol; 517 mg Sodium. Exchanges: 0 Grain (Starch); 0 Lean Meat; 1 Vegetable; 1 Fat; 1/2 Other Carbohydrates.

Broccoli and Rice Casserole

2 (10-ounce) packages frozen chopped broccoli

1 cup uncooked rice

Salt to taste

2 cups water

1/2 cup (1 stick) margarine, melted

1 onion, grated

1 (10-ounce) can cream of mushroom soup

1/2 cup milk

1 (8-ounce) jar Cheez Whiz

Buttered bread crumbs

- Cook the broccoli in a saucepan using the package directions; drain. Cook the rice in salted water in a saucepan until the rice is tender and the water is absorbed.

- Mix the margarine, onion, soup, milk and Cheez Whiz in a large bowl. Add the broccoli and rice and mix well. Spoon into a large baking dish. Sprinkle with buttered bread crumbs.

- Bake at 350 degrees for 20 to 25 minutes or until bubbly.

YIELD: 6 TO 8 SERVINGS

After a massive fire, which devastated the Courthouse, the voters of Jefferson County held a special election on April 12, 1977, and voted 7,531 to 733 to restore the Courthouse at its original site. The plans, which included the original center section and bell tower, were drawn up by the firm of Reed, Willis and Burks, and construction was completed by the Richardson Construction Company of North Little Rock just in time for the county's 150th anniversary. A parade and addresses by prominent citizens marked the opening of the new building on May 8, 1980.

Carrot Casserole

2 cups mashed cooked carrots
1/2 cup (1 stick) margarine, melted
3 eggs, beaten
1/2 cup sugar
1 tablespoon flour
1 teaspoon baking powder
1/4 teaspoon cinnamon

- Combine the carrots, margarine, eggs, sugar, flour, baking powder and cinnamon in a bowl and mix well. Pour into a buttered baking dish.
- Bake at 400 degrees for 15 minutes. Reduce the heat to 325 degrees. Bake for 35 minutes or until bubbly.

YIELD: 4 TO 6 SERVINGS

Maple-Glazed Carrots

1 pound baby carrots
2 tablespoons butter
1 tablespoon maple syrup

- Cook the carrots in boiling water in a saucepan for 15 minutes or until tender. Drain the carrots in a colander and return to the saucepan.
- Stir in the butter and maple syrup. Serve immediately.

YIELD: 4 TO 6 SERVINGS

Raspberry Carrots

1 pound baby carrots

3 tablespoons butter

1 tablespoon raspberry vinegar

2 teaspoons brown sugar

Salt to taste

Chopped fresh tarragon to taste

• Process the carrots in a food processor until grated. Sauté the carrots in the butter in a skillet until tender. Add the vinegar and brown sugar and toss gently to coat. Cook for a few more minutes. Season with salt. Sprinkle with tarragon just before serving.

YIELD: 4 TO 6 SERVINGS

Saucy Carrots

8 to 10 carrots

1/4 teaspoon salt

2 tablespoons prepared mustard

1/4 cup packed brown sugar

1 tablespoon light corn syrup

2 tablespoons margarine

• Cut the carrots into slices. Cook the carrots in boiling salted water in a saucepan until tender; drain.

• Combine the mustard, brown sugar, corn syrup and margarine in a saucepan and mix well. Cook until the brown sugar and margarine melt, stirring constantly. Pour over the carrots and toss to coat.

Note: You may use a package of baby carrots.

YIELD: 6 TO 8 SERVINGS

Grilled Corn on the Cob

1/2 cup (1 stick) butter or margarine, softened
1 teaspoon salt
1/2 teaspoon crushed rosemary
1/2 teaspoon crushed marjoram
6 ears of corn

- Cream the butter and salt in a mixing bowl until fluffy. Add a mixture of the rosemary and marjoram and mix well. Let stand at room temperature for 1 hour to enhance the flavors.

- Turn back the husks of the corn. Remove the silks with a stiff brush. Place each ear of corn on a piece of heavy-duty foil. Spread each ear of corn with 1 tablespoon of the butter mixture. Lay the husks back into position and wrap securely in the foil.

- Arrange on a grill rack. Grill over hot coals for 12 to 15 minutes or until the corn is tender, turning frequently.

YIELD: 6 SERVINGS

Rich and Creamy Corn

2 (11-ounce) cans white Shoe Peg corn, drained
1/2 cup (1 stick) butter
8 ounces cream cheese, chopped
1/2 (4-ounce) can green chiles, drained

- Combine the corn, butter, cream cheese and green chiles in a medium saucepan and mix well.

- Cook over medium heat for 20 minutes or until the butter and cream cheese melt, stirring frequently.

Note: You may double this recipe.

YIELD: 8 TO 10 SERVINGS

Corn Pudding

2 tablespoons chopped green bell pepper

2 tablespoons chopped onion

2 tablespoons butter

2 tablespoons chopped pimento

3 tablespoons flour

1 teaspoon salt

1/4 teaspoon pepper

Garlic salt and seasoned salt to taste

2 (16-ounce) cans cream-style corn

1/4 cup milk

2 eggs, lightly beaten

- Combine the bell pepper, onion and butter in an 1 1/2-quart microwave-safe dish and mix well.

- Microwave on Medium until the onion is transparent. Stir in the pimento.

- Add the flour, salt, pepper, garlic salt, seasoned salt, corn, milk and eggs and mix well.

- Microwave, covered, on Medium for 9 minutes and stir. Microwave, uncovered, for 7 to 8 minutes or until the mixture is slightly soft. Let stand for 5 minutes before serving.

YIELD: 6 TO 8 SERVINGS

Corn and Okra Medley

3 cups water

3 ears of fresh corn

4 slices bacon

1 small onion, chopped

1 pound fresh okra, sliced

1 large tomato, seeded and chopped

1 teaspoon salt

1 teaspoon pepper

- Bring the water to a boil in a large saucepan. Add the corn. Return to a boil and reduce the heat. Simmer for 10 to 12 minutes or until the corn is tender. Drain and rinse in cold water. Pat dry with paper towels. Cut the corn from the cob into a bowl, scraping the cob to remove the juices.

- Cook the bacon in a large skillet over medium heat until crisp. Remove the bacon with a slotted spoon to paper towels to drain, reserving the drippings in the skillet. Crumble the bacon.

- Sauté the onion in the reserved drippings until tender. Add the okra. Cook for 5 minutes, stirring occasionally. Stir in the tomato and corn.

- Cook over low heat for 5 to 7 minutes, stirring occasionally. Season with the salt and pepper. Sprinkle with the bacon.

YIELD: 6 SERVINGS

Per Serving (excluding unknown items): 104 Calories; 3 g Fat (22.3% calories from fat); 5 g Protein; 17 g Carbohydrate; 4 mg Cholesterol; 442 mg Sodium. Exchanges: 1/2 Grain (Starch); 0 Lean Meat; 1 1/2 Vegetable; 1/2 Fat.

Corn and Green Bean Casserole

1 (11-ounce) can white Shoe Peg corn, drained
1 (16-ounce) can French-style green beans, drained
1/2 cup finely chopped onion
1/2 cup finely chopped celery
2 cups (8 ounces) shredded Cheddar cheese
1/2 cup sour cream
1 (10-ounce) can cream of celery soup
Salt and pepper to taste
1/4 cup (1/2 stick) butter
1 sleeve butter crackers

- Combine the corn, green beans, onion, celery, cheese, sour cream, soup, salt and pepper in a bowl and mix well. Spoon into a greased 2-quart baking dish.

- Bake at 350 degrees for 30 minutes.

- Melt the butter in a small saucepan. Crumble the crackers into a bowl. Add the melted butter and mix well. Sprinkle over the corn mixture.

- Bake for 15 minutes longer.

YIELD: 6 TO 8 SERVINGS

Green Beans with Roasted Onions

6 medium onions

4 tablespoons butter

Salt and pepper to taste

2 cups canned low-salt chicken broth

3 tablespoons sugar

2 tablespoons red wine vinegar

3 pounds slender green beans, trimmed

1 tablespoon salt

2 tablespoons butter

- Cut each of the onions vertically through the root end into 12 to 14 wedges. Arrange in a single layer on 2 large heavy baking sheets sprayed with nonstick cooking spray. Dot with 4 tablespoons butter. Season with salt and pepper to taste.

- Bake at 450 degrees for 35 minutes or until the onions are dark brown on the bottom.

- Boil the broth in a large heavy skillet over high heat for 6 minutes or until reduced to 1/2 cup. Add the sugar and vinegar. Whisk until the sugar dissolves and the mixture comes to a boil. Stir in the onions. Reduce the heat to medium-low.

- Simmer for 5 minutes or until the liquid is slightly reduced. Season with salt and pepper. (You may prepare 1 day ahead up to this point. Cover and refrigerate. Reheat over low heat before continuing.)

- Cook the green beans seasoned with 1 tablespoon salt in water to cover in a large saucepan for 5 minutes or until tender-crisp. Drain and return the green beans to the saucepan. Add 2 tablespoons butter and toss to coat.

- Mound the green beans in a large shallow bowl. Top with the onion mixture and serve.

YIELD: 6 TO 8 SERVINGS

Portobello Mushrooms Stuffed with Artichoke Hearts

4 portobello mushrooms, stems removed

1 (14-ounce) can artichoke hearts, drained and chopped

2 green onions, chopped

1 tablespoon minced fresh parsley

1/4 teaspoon garlic powder

1/4 cup grated Parmesan cheese

3 tablespoons sour cream

2 tablespoons Italian bread crumbs

Salt and pepper to taste

1/2 cup (2 ounces) shredded smoked Gouda cheese

- Clean the mushrooms. Mix the artichoke hearts, green onions, parsley, garlic powder, Parmesan cheese, sour cream and bread crumbs in a bowl and mix well. Season with salt and pepper.

- Stuff the mushrooms with the artichoke mixture. Sprinkle with the Gouda cheese. Arrange in a 9×13-inch baking pan.

- Bake at 350 degrees for 15 to 20 minutes or until the mushrooms are tender.

YIELD: 4 SERVINGS

Per Serving (excluding unknown items): 202 Calories; 9 g Fat (35.4 % calories from fat); 13 g Protein; 22 g Carbohydrate; 24 mg Cholesterol; 422 mg Sodium. Exchanges: 0 Grain (Starch); 1 Lean Meat; 3 1/2 Vegetable; 0 Non-Fat Milk; 1 Fat.

Sweet Onion Casserole

1 to 2 sweet onions, such as Texas 1015 or Vidalia

1 (10-ounce) can creamy chicken mushroom soup

1 cup (4 ounces) shredded American or Cheddar cheese

1/2 cup corn flakes, crushed

- Grease a 9×13-inch baking dish with butter or nonstick cooking spray. Cut the onions into slices.

- Layer the onions in the prepared dish. Spread the soup over the onions. Sprinkle with the cheese and corn flakes.

- Bake at 350 degrees for 45 minutes.

YIELD: 6 TO 8 SERVINGS

Pineapple Casserole

2 (20-ounce) cans pineapple chunks

1 cup sugar

5 tablespoons flour

1 1/2 cups (6 ounces) shredded mild Cheddar cheese

1 1/2 cups butter cracker crumbs

1/2 cup (1 stick) butter, melted

- Drain the pineapple, discarding the liquid. Layer the pineapple in a greased baking dish. Sprinkle with the sugar, flour and cheese.

- Mix the cracker crumbs with the butter in a bowl. Sprinkle over the top.

- Bake at 350 degrees for 45 minutes.

YIELD: 6 TO 8 SERVINGS

Onion Hands

If you have an aluminum sink, you can eliminate the onion smell from your hands by simply rubbing your hands around on your sink.

Scooter's Custard-Top Fresh Corn Spoon Bread

Tori and Eric Klein, sous chef for Spago Beverly Hills, have a dear friend, Scooter Kanfer, known for her interesting spoon breads at her restaurant, the house, located in Los Angeles. She serves them in individual cast-iron skillets made especially for her.

2 cups flour

1^1/2 cups stone-ground cornmeal

2 teaspoons baking powder

1 teaspoon baking soda

10 ears of fresh corn

Minced fresh marjoram to taste

4 eggs

4 cups milk

^{1}/2 cup (1 stick) butter, melted

5 tablespoons sugar

3 tablespoons apple cider vinegar

1 teaspoon kosher salt

1 teaspoon freshly ground pepper

2 cups heavy cream

- Mix the flour, cornmeal, baking powder and baking soda in a large metal bowl. Scrape the corn from the cob into a bowl, running the back of your chef's knife down the cob to scrape off any extra bits and to get any liquid that remains. Add the corn and marjoram to the flour mixture and mix well.

- Whisk the eggs in a large bowl. Add the milk, butter, sugar, vinegar, kosher salt and pepper and mix well. Add the corn mixture and stir gently by hand until mixed. Do not use an electric mixer. Do not overbeat. (Treat the dough gently and the spoon bread will be tender and light.)

- Pour into a large buttered and sugared baking dish. Pour the cream over the top. Do not stir in the cream.

- Bake at 350 degrees for 1 hour or until puffed and golden brown. Remove from the oven. Let stand for at least 10 minutes before serving.

YIELD: 15 TO 20 SERVINGS

Hash Brown Potato Casserole

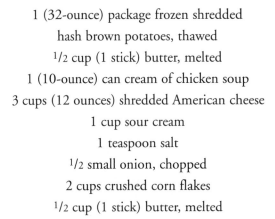

1 (32-ounce) package frozen shredded
hash brown potatoes, thawed
1/2 cup (1 stick) butter, melted
1 (10-ounce) can cream of chicken soup
3 cups (12 ounces) shredded American cheese
1 cup sour cream
1 teaspoon salt
1/2 small onion, chopped
2 cups crushed corn flakes
1/2 cup (1 stick) butter, melted

• Layer the potatoes in a 9×13-inch baking dish. Combine 1/2 cup butter, soup, cheese, sour cream, salt and onion in a bowl and mix well. Pour evenly over the potatoes. Sprinkle the crushed corn flakes over the top. Drizzle with 1/2 cup melted butter.

• Bake at 350 degrees for 45 minutes.

YIELD: 12 SERVINGS

Roasted Garlic Mashed Potatoes

2 large garlic bulbs

2 tablespoons olive oil

3 pounds russet potatoes, peeled and quartered

2 tablespoons olive oil

1/4 cup (1/2 stick) unsalted butter

1/2 teaspoon coarse salt

1/2 teaspoon coarsely ground pepper

- Place the whole unpeeled garlic bulbs in a small baking pan. Drizzle with 2 tablespoons olive oil. Place on the center oven rack. Bake at 350 degrees for 30 to 40 minutes or until the bulbs feel soft when gently squeezed. Remove from the oven. Let stand for 15 minutes to cool.

- Place the potatoes in a saucepan and cover with water. Bring to a boil. Boil, covered, for 30 minutes or until tender; drain.

- Mash the potatoes in a medium bowl with a potato masher or fork. Add 2 tablespoons olive oil, butter, salt and pepper and mix well. Cut the garlic bulbs into halves horizontally. Squeeze the soft garlic pulp into the mashed potatoes and mix well.

Yield: 6 servings

New Potato Casserole

10 new potatoes

1/2 cup (1 stick) butter

8 ounces cream cheese

2 tablespoons real bacon bits

1 (2-ounce) jar sliced green olives with pimentos, drained

1 cup (4 ounces) shredded Cheddar cheese

Chopped scallions

- Peel the potatoes and cut into quarters. Place in a saucepan and cover with water. Bring to a boil. Boil for 5 minutes; drain. Arrange in a 9×9-inch baking dish.

- Melt the butter and cream cheese in a saucepan over low heat, stirring constantly. Add the bacon bits and olives and mix well. Pour over the potatoes. Sprinkle with the Cheddar cheese and scallions.

- Bake at 350 degrees for 30 minutes.

YIELD: 8 SERVINGS

Sinful Potatoes

12 ounces sliced bacon

2 pounds frozen hash brown potatoes

1 pound Velveeta cheese

1 cup mayonnaise

1 cup sour cream

1/4 teaspoon cayenne pepper

1 bunch green onions, finely chopped

- Cook the bacon in a skillet until tender-crisp; drain. Crumble the bacon into small pieces. Thaw the potatoes for 15 minutes.

- Melt the cheese in a heavy saucepan over low heat. Combine the cheese, mayonnaise, sour cream, cayenne pepper and potatoes in a large bowl and mix well.

- Spread the green onions in a well-greased baking pan. Layer the potato mixture over the green onions. Sprinkle the bacon over the top.

- Bake at 350 degrees for 35 to 40 minutes or until bubbly and cooked through.

Note: You may assemble this recipe and freeze until ready to bake.
Bake at 350 degrees for 1 hour.

YIELD: 12 SERVINGS

Per Serving (excluding unknown items): 226 Calories; 14 g Fat (57.6% calories from fat); 10 g Protein; 14 g Carbohydrate; 24 mg Cholesterol; 470 mg Sodium. Exchanges: 1 Grain (Starch); 1 Lean Meat; 0 Vegetable; 2 Fat.

Squash Excellente

2 cups yellow squash (about 4 large squash)

1 tablespoon bacon drippings

Salt and lemon pepper to taste

Pinch of sugar

1 tablespoon sweet basil

1 medium onion, chopped

1 cup fresh mushrooms, sliced

3 tablespoons butter

3/4 cup cooked rice

1 cup crumbled cheese crackers

1 (10-ounce) can cream of mushroom soup

1/2 cup milk

1/3 cup sliced water chestnuts

- Combine the squash, bacon drippings, salt, lemon pepper, sugar and basil in a saucepan. Add enough water to cover. Cook until the squash is tender; drain. Mash the squash mixture.

- Sauté the onion and mushrooms in the butter in a skillet. Combine with the squash mixture and rice in a large bowl and mix well. Add 1/2 cup of the cracker crumbs, soup, milk and water chestnuts and mix well. Pour into a greased 9×13-inch baking dish. Sprinkle with the remaining cracker crumbs.

- Bake at 350 degrees for 30 to 45 minutes or until heated through.

YIELD: 6 TO 8 SERVINGS

Parmesan-Glazed Tomatoes

3 medium tomatoes

Salt and freshly ground pepper to taste

3 tablespoons mayonnaise

2 tablespoons grated Parmesan cheese

1 teaspoon Dijon mustard

1 tablespoon finely chopped fresh parsley

2 teaspoons finely snipped fresh chives, or

2/3 teaspoon dried chives

1/4 teaspoon garlic powder

1 tablespoon grated Parmesan cheese

1 tablespoon finely chopped fresh parsley

- Peel the tomatoes and cut into 3/4-inch slices. Arrange the tomatoes in a single layer in a nonreactive baking pan. Season with salt and pepper to taste.

- Combine the mayonnaise, 2 tablespoons cheese, Dijon mustard, 1 tablespoon parsley, chives and garlic powder in a small bowl and mix well. Spread over the tomatoes. Sprinkle with 1 tablespoon cheese.

- Bake at 400 degrees for 10 minutes or until heated through. Turn on the broiler. Broil 4 to 6 inches from the heat source for 2 minutes or until the topping is golden and bubbly. Sprinkle with 1 tablespoon parsley.

YIELD: 6 SERVINGS

Freezer Tomatoes
If you have tomatoes that are too ripe to eat, this is a great way to save them for soups and sauces in the winter. Use firm, ripe tomatoes. Rinse and remove the core, but do not peel. Place the whole tomatoes on a baking sheet and freeze. Store in sealable plastic freezer bags until ready to use.

Creamed Lemon Spinach

4 slices bacon

1 medium onion, chopped

2 garlic cloves, minced

3 tablespoons flour

1^1/$_2$ cups milk

2 (10-ounce) packages frozen chopped spinach,
thawed and squeezed dry

2 tablespoons fresh lemon juice

1 teaspoon grated lemon zest

1/4 cup grated Parmesan cheese

Salt and pepper to taste

- Cook the bacon in a large heavy skillet over medium heat until tender-crisp. Remove to paper towels to drain, reserving the drippings in the skillet.

- Add the onion and garlic to the reserved bacon drippings in the skillet.

- Sauté over medium heat for 6 minutes or until tender. Add the flour.

- Cook for 2 minutes, stirring constantly. Whisk in the milk gradually. Increase the heat to high.

- Cook for 2 minutes or until the sauce thickens and comes to a boil, whisking constantly. Reduce the heat to low. Add the spinach, lemon juice and lemon zest.

- Cook until heated through, stirring constantly. Stir in the cheese and crumbled bacon. Season with salt and pepper to taste.

Note: This is a great accompaniment to prime rib, pork chops or veal.

YIELD: 6 SERVINGS

Spinach, Mushroom and Artichoke Casserole

2 (16-ounce) packages frozen chopped spinach
1/4 cup (1/2 stick) butter
8 ounces sliced fresh mushrooms (3 cups)
1/2 cup onion, finely chopped
1 (14- or 16-ounce) can artichoke hearts, drained and chopped
1/2 cup light mayonnaise
1/2 cup light sour cream
1/2 teaspoon salt
1/8 teaspoon white pepper
5 teaspoons fresh lemon juice
1/2 cup grated Parmesan cheese

- Cook the spinach using the package directions; drain. Squeeze the excess liquid from the spinach.

- Melt the butter in a 10-inch skillet. Add the mushrooms and onion. Sauté until tender.

- Combine the spinach, sautéed mushroom mixture, artichoke hearts, mayonnaise, sour cream, salt, white pepper, lemon juice and 1/4 cup of the cheese in a bowl and mix well. Spoon into a 2 1/2-quart baking dish sprayed with nonstick cooking spray. Sprinkle with the remaining 1/4 cup cheese.

- Bake at 350 degrees for 20 to 30 minutes or until bubbly and light brown.

Note: This recipe may be doubled and frozen. Thaw before baking.

YIELD: 6 SERVINGS

Florentine Supreme

1 (10-ounce) package frozen chopped spinach
3/4 cup seasoned dry bread crumbs
1/2 cup finely chopped green onions
3 eggs, lightly beaten
6 tablespoons butter, melted
1/3 cup grated Parmesan cheese
4 slices bacon, crisp-cooked and crumbled
Salt and pepper to taste
Grated Parmesan cheese to taste

• Cook the spinach using the package directions; drain. Combine the spinach, bread crumbs, green onions, eggs, butter, 1/3 cup Parmesan cheese, crumbled bacon and salt and pepper in a large bowl and mix well. Spoon into a greased 9×12-inch baking dish. Sprinkle with cheese to taste.

• Bake at 350 degrees for 20 minutes.

YIELD: 4 TO 6 SERVINGS

Mashed Sweet Potatoes with Maple Syrup

2 1/4 pounds red-skinned sweet potatoes
Salt to taste
1/4 cup (1/2 stick) butter
2 tablespoons pure maple syrup
1/2 teaspoon cardamom
Pepper to taste

- Peel the sweet potatoes and cut into 1-inch pieces. Place the sweet potatoes in a saucepan and cover with water. Season with salt. Bring to a boil. Boil for 20 minutes or until the sweet potatoes are tender; drain. Return the sweet potatoes to the saucepan.

- Mash the sweet potatoes. Add the butter, maple syrup and cardamom and mix well. Season with salt and pepper to taste.

Note: Works beautifully with pork.

YIELD: 4 SERVINGS

The Saenger Theatre
Built in 1924 at the cost of $350,000, the Saenger was one of the premiere theatres built in the Southeast. Prominent guests and performers have included noted film producer, D. W. Griffith; silent film actress, Norma Talmadge; John Phillip Sousa's Military Band; George White's SCANDALS; Houdini; Tom Mix and His Wonder Horse, Tony; Will Rogers; Douglas Fairbanks, Jr.; Geraldine Chaplin and the Zoppe Circus; and Van Johnson. A victim of a deteriorating downtown base, the Saenger closed its doors in 1975. Still standing, the theatre boasts of a full-sized Broadway stage and the fly loft is seven stories high. Its lobby is floored with black and white marble imported from Italy. Now owned by the Old Towne Theatre Center, the Saenger is one of the last remaining grand theatres.

137

Sweet Potato Soufflé

6 small sweet potatoes

3/4 cup sugar

3 eggs, lightly beaten

1/2 cup (1 stick) butter, melted

3 tablespoons milk

1 1/2 teaspoons cinnamon

1/2 teaspoon ground nutmeg

2 teaspoons vanilla extract

3/4 teaspoon lemon extract

- Peel the sweet potatoes and cut into pieces. Place in a saucepan and cover with water. Bring to a boil. Boil for 15 to 20 minutes or until tender; drain. Mash the sweet potatoes.

- Add the sugar, eggs, butter, milk, cinnamon, nutmeg, vanilla and lemon extract and mix well. Spoon into a lightly greased 7×11-inch baking dish.

- Bake at 350 degrees for 30 minutes or until bubbly.

YIELD: 6 SERVINGS

Per Serving (excluding unknown items): 414 Calories; 18 g Fat (39.3% calories from fat); 5 g Protein; 58 g Carbohydrate; 136 mg Cholesterol; 205 mg Sodium. Exchanges: 2 Grain (Starch); 1/2 Lean Meat; 0 Non-Fat Milk; 3 1/2 Fat; 1 1/2 Other Carbohydrates.

Oven-Roasted Vegetables

$1/3$ cup olive oil

2 to 3 tablespoons fresh rosemary, thyme, basil or herbes de Provence

Carrots, cut into 2-inch pieces

Zucchini, cut diagonally into pieces $1/2$ inch thick

Sweet potatoes, cut into pieces $1/2$ inch thick

Bell peppers, cut into 2-inch pieces

Asparagus, trimmed

Onions, cut into quarters

Eggplant, cut diagonally into $1/2$-inch slices

Salt to taste

- Combine the olive oil and rosemary in a bowl and mix well. Let stand for 1 hour or longer before using.

- Combine the carrots, zucchini, sweet potatoes, bell peppers, asparagus, onions and eggplant or your favorite combination of the vegetables in a large bowl. Add the olive oil mixture and toss to coat well. Arrange in a single layer in a shallow roasting pan. Sprinkle with salt.

- Bake at 500 degrees for 8 minutes. Reduce the oven temperature to 400 degrees. Bake for 6 to 8 minutes or until the vegetables are tender when pierced with a knife.

YIELD: VARIABLE

Chiles Rellenos Casserole

4 cups (16 ounces) shredded Monterey Jack cheese

4 cups (16 ounces) shredded Cheddar cheese

2 (7-ounce) cans chopped green chiles, drained

3 eggs, beaten

3 tablespoons flour

1 (5-ounce) can evaporated milk

1 (15-ounce) can tomato sauce

- Reserve 1/4 cup each of the Monterey Jack cheese and Cheddar cheese. Layer the green chiles, the remaining Monterey Jack cheese and the remaining Cheddar cheese 1/2 at a time in a 9×13-inch greased baking pan.

- Beat the eggs in a mixing bowl until fluffy. Add the flour and evaporated milk and mix well. Pour over the layers.

- Bake at 350 degrees for 30 minutes. Spread the tomato sauce over the top. Sprinkle with the reserved Monterey Jack cheese and Cheddar cheese. Bake for 15 minutes longer.

Note: You may prepare ahead and chill, covered, before baking.

YIELD: 6 TO 8 SERVINGS

Vegetarian Enchilada Casserole

1 medium onion, chopped
1 garlic clove, minced
Vegetable oil for sautéing
2 (15-ounce) cans pinto beans, drained
2 (8-ounce) cans tomato sauce
1 envelope taco seasoning mix
1 (4-ounce) can chopped green chiles, drained
1 (2-ounce) can sliced black olives, drained
1 cup (4 ounces) reduced-fat shredded cheese
2 1/2 cups reduced-fat cottage cheese
1 (10-ounce) package corn tortillas, cut into quarters

- Sauté the onion and garlic in a small amount of vegetable oil in a skillet until tender. Add the beans, tomato sauce and taco seasoning mix and mix well. Stir in the green chiles and black olives. Simmer for 5 minutes.

- Spread 1/3 of the bean mixture in a 9×13-inch baking dish. Layer the cheese, cottage cheese, tortillas and remaining bean mixture 1/2 at a time in the prepared dish, ending with the bean mixture.

- Bake, covered, at 350 degrees for 25 minutes. Garnish with sliced olives and chopped tomatoes.

YIELD: 6 TO 8 SERVINGS

Don't Waste the Tomato Paste
In recipes that call for just a bit of tomato paste, you can substitute ketchup. You cannot tell the difference and there is no need to waste a whole can of tomato paste.

Orzo Parsley Gratin

16 ounces uncooked orzo (rice-shaped pasta)

6 garlic cloves

Salt to taste

1 cup heavy cream

1 cup canned chicken broth

3/4 cup freshly grated Parmesan cheese

1 cup minced fresh parsley leaves

Pepper to taste

1/4 cup dry bread crumbs

1/4 cup freshly grated Parmesan cheese

1/4 cup minced fresh parsley leaves

3 tablespoons cold unsalted butter, thinly sliced

- Boil the orzo and unpeeled garlic cloves in salted water in a large saucepan for 10 minutes or until al dente; drain in a colander. Rinse the orzo well under cold water and drain again. Remove the garlic cloves and peel.

- Mash the garlic in a large bowl using a fork. Whisk in the cream. Add the orzo, broth, 3/4 cup cheese, 1 cup parsley and salt and pepper to taste; mix well. Spoon into a buttered 2-quart baking dish and smooth the top.

- Toss the bread crumbs with 1/4 cup cheese and 1/4 cup parsley in a bowl. Sprinkle evenly over the orzo mixture. Dot the top with the butter.

- Bake, uncovered, at 325 degrees for 1 1/4 hours or until bubbly around the edges and golden brown on top.

YIELD: 10 SERVINGS

Asparagus Lemon Pasta

1 1/2 pounds asparagus

Salt to taste

20 cups (5 quarts) water

16 ounces bow tie pasta

3 tablespoons unsalted butter

3/4 cup heavy cream

1/4 cup fresh lemon juice

2 tablespoons freshly grated lemon zest
(from about 3 lemons)

3/4 teaspoon salt

1/3 cup finely chopped fresh parsley
leaves

Pepper to taste

Freshly grated Parmesan cheese

- Trim the asparagus and cut diagonally into slices 1/2 inch thick. Steam, covered, in a steamer over boiling water for 3 minutes or until tender crisp. Remove to a colander to drain. Rinse under cold water to stop the cooking process; drain well.

- Bring 20 cups of salted water to a boil in a large saucepan. Add the pasta. Cook until al dente, stirring occasionally.

- Heat the butter and cream in a deep 12-inch skillet over medium-low heat until the butter melts. Stir in the lemon juice, lemon zest and 3/4 teaspoon salt. Remove from the heat and cover to keep warm.

- Drain the pasta, reserving 1/4 cup of the water. Add the reserved pasta water to the lemon sauce and mix well. Add the pasta and asparagus.

- Cover over medium heat for 1 minute or until heated through, tossing constantly to mix well. Add the parsley and salt and pepper to taste and toss to mix well. Sprinkle with cheese.

Note: Turn this side dish into an entrée by adding chicken. To prepare the chicken, season boneless skinless chicken breasts with Italian seasoning. Pour 1/2 cup dry white wine into a shallow baking dish. Arrange the chicken in a single layer in the wine. Bake, covered, at 350 degrees for 15 minutes or until the liquid is absorbed and the chicken is cooked through. Cool the chicken. Cut into small pieces and add to the pasta at the same time the asparagus is added.

YIELD: 6 TO 8 SERVINGS

Pasta Sauce Raphael

2 (6-ounce) jars marinated artichoke hearts

1/4 cup olive oil

2 cups chopped onions

2 tablespoons minced garlic

1/2 teaspoon oregano

1/2 teaspoon basil

1 tablespoon coarsely ground pepper

1/2 teaspoon salt

Pinch of red pepper flakes

1 (28-ounce) can plum tomatoes

1/4 cup freshly grated Parmesan cheese

1/4 cup chopped fresh Italian flat-leaf parsley

- Drain the artichoke hearts, reserving the marinade.

- Heat the olive oil in a large saucepan. Add the onions, garlic, oregano, basil, pepper, salt, red pepper flakes and reserved marinade.

- Sauté over medium-low heat for 10 minutes or until the onions and garlic are soft and translucent. Add the tomatoes.

- Simmer for 30 minutes. Add the artichoke hearts, cheese and parsley.

- Simmer for 5 minutes, stirring gently.

Note: This sauce is especially good served over hot cooked tortellini.

YIELD: 6 SERVINGS

Paprika Rice

5 cups water

2$\frac{1}{2}$ cups long grain rice

Salt to taste

2 teaspoons paprika

- Bring the water, rice and salt to a boil in a kettle over high heat. Reduce the heat.
- Simmer, covered, for 20 to 25 minutes or until the rice is fluffy and dry. Add the paprika and toss to coat. Spoon into a serving bowl.

YIELD: 8 SERVINGS

Parslied Rice

2 cups long grain rice

4 cups (1 quart) water

1 tablespoon salt

2 tablespoons butter

1 cup minced fresh parsley

- Place the rice, water, salt and butter in a large saucepan. Bring to a boil over medium-high heat. Reduce the heat to low.
- Cook, covered, for 20 minutes or until the rice is fluffy and dry.
- Combine the rice and parsley in a large bowl and toss to mix well.

YIELD: 8 TO 10 SERVINGS

Shelling Peas

To make your pea shelling easier, drop the pods into a saucepan of boiling water. The pods will split open and the peas will float to the surface. You can then just skim the shelled peas off the surface of the water.

145

Wild Rice with Pecans

2 tablespoons butter or margarine
2 (6-ounce) packages long grain and wild rice mix
4 cups chicken broth
8 green onions, chopped
8 medium mushrooms, sliced
1^1/$_2$ cups chopped pecans, toasted

- Melt the butter in a large Dutch oven. Add the rice.

- Cook over medium heat until light brown, stirring frequently. Stir in the rice seasoning packets, broth, green onions and mushrooms.

- Bring to a boil and remove from the heat. Pour into a lightly greased 3-quart baking dish.

- Bake, covered, at 350 degrees for 30 minutes. Bake, uncovered, for 30 minutes longer or until the rice is tender and the liquid is absorbed, stirring after 15 minutes. Stir in the pecans.

YIELD: 12 SERVINGS

Poultry & Seafood

The Governor Mike Huckabee Delta Rivers Nature Center

The Delta Rivers Nature Center—

conserving our natural resources

through exposure, experience, and education.

Aquariums, live animals, nature trails,

and interactive exhibits all help the visitor to

learn more about Arkansas' Delta region.

SPONSOR

Baked Chicken with Creamy Dijon Sauce

1 egg

1 tablespoon Dijon mustard

4 boneless skinless chicken breasts

$1/4$ cup flour

$1/2$ cup garlic and herb seasoned bread crumbs

2 tablespoons half-and-half

2 teaspoons Dijon mustard

$1/2$ teaspoon sugar

2 teaspoons chopped fresh parsley, or to taste

- Beat the egg and 1 tablespoon Dijon mustard in a shallow bowl until blended. Coat the chicken with the flour. Dip in the egg mixture and then in the bread crumbs to coat. Arrange the chicken in an 8×8-inch baking pan sprayed with nonstick cooking spray. Spray lightly with nonstick cooking spray.

- Bake at 400 degrees for 18 to 20 minutes or until the juices run clear.

- Combine the half-and-half, 2 teaspoons Dijon mustard and sugar in a small bowl and mix well. Drizzle over the baked chicken. Sprinkle with the parsley.

YIELD: 4 SERVINGS

Chicken and Dumplings

1 hen

4 ribs celery

1 small onion

2 carrots

1 tablespoon salt

1 1/2 cups flour

1/2 teaspoon salt

3 tablespoons shortening

1 egg, beaten

5 tablespoons water

- Place the hen, celery, onion, carrots and 1 tablespoon salt in a large stockpot. Add enough water to barely cover. Bring to a boil. Boil for 1 1/2 hours. Remove the hen to a platter to cool.

- Strain the broth, discarding the solids. Return the broth to the stockpot. Cook until the broth is reduced by half.

- Mix the flour and 1/2 teaspoon salt in a bowl. Cut in the shortening until crumbly. Stir in the egg and water. Add additional water if needed to form a thin dough. Divide the dough into 3 equal portions. Roll each portion into a very thin rectangle on a lightly floured surface. Let stand for 30 minutes. Cut into strips 1 1/2 inches wide. Drop into the simmering broth. Cook, covered for 20 minutes.

- Shred the hen, discarding the skin and bones. Stir into the dumplings.

YIELD: 8 SERVINGS

Stuffed Chicken Breasts with Artichoke Hearts

1 teaspoon olive oil	4 boneless skinless chicken breasts
3/4 cup frozen artichoke hearts, thawed and chopped	1 teaspoon olive oil
1/4 cup minced shallots	1/8 teaspoon salt
1/4 cup crumbled feta cheese	1/8 teaspoon pepper
1/2 teaspoon thyme	1/2 teaspoon thyme
1/8 teaspoon salt	1 cup fat-free chicken broth
1/8 teaspoon pepper	2 tablespoons fresh lemon juice
	2 teaspoons cornstarch

- Heat 1 teaspoon olive oil in a nonstick skillet over medium heat. Add the artichoke hearts and shallots. Sauté for 4 minutes. Remove to a bowl to cool. Stir in the cheese, 1/2 teaspoon thyme, 1/8 teaspoon salt and 1/8 teaspoon pepper.

- Cut a horizontal slit through the thickest portion of each chicken breast to form a pocket. Stuff 2 tablespoons of the artichoke mixture into each pocket.

- Heat 1 teaspoon olive oil in a large nonstick skillet over medium heat. Add the chicken. Sprinkle with 1/8 teaspoon salt and 1/8 teaspoon pepper. Sauté for 6 minutes on each side or until the chicken is cooked through. Remove from the skillet to a plate and keep warm, reserving the drippings in the skillet.

- Add 1/2 teaspoon thyme and broth to the drippings in the skillet. Bring to a boil. Mix the lemon juice and cornstarch in a small bowl. Whisk into the broth mixture. Cook for 1 minute or until thickened, stirring constantly. Return the chicken to the skillet. Cook, covered, for 2 minutes or until heated through. Garnish with fresh parsley and lemon rind strips.

YIELD: 4 SERVINGS

Per Serving (excluding unknown items): 215 Calories; 6 g Fat (24.8% calories from fat); 33 g Protein; 8 g Carbohydrate; 77 mg Cholesterol; 470 mg Sodium. Exchanges: 0 Grain (Starch); 4 1/2 Lean Meat; 1 Vegetable; 0 Fruit; 1/2 Fat.

Sautéed Chicken in Lemon Cream Sauce

6 boneless skinless chicken breasts

Salt and pepper to taste

1/4 cup (1/2 stick) butter

2 tablespoons dry vermouth

2 tablespoons fresh lemon juice

2 teaspoons grated lemon zest

3/4 cup whipping cream

1/2 cup reduced-sodium chicken broth

1/2 cup grated Parmesan cheese

- Place the chicken between sheets of plastic wrap. Pound the chicken lightly until 1/2 inch thick using a meat mallet. Season with salt and pepper.

- Melt the butter in a large heavy skillet over medium-high heat. Add the chicken. Sauté for 3 minutes per side or until cooked through. Remove the chicken to a platter. Cover with foil to keep warm.

- Drain the butter from the skillet. Add the vermouth, lemon juice and lemon zest to the skillet. Boil for 1 minute, stirring to deglaze the skillet. Add the cream, broth and any juices accumulated from the chicken. Boil for 8 minutes or until the mixture is reduced to a sauce consistency. Stir in 1/4 cup of the cheese. Season with salt and pepper.

- Pour the sauce around the chicken. Sprinkle with the remaining 1/4 cup cheese. Garnish with chopped fresh parsley and lemon wedges.

YIELD: 6 SERVINGS

Marinade for Chicken

Combine 1 cup olive oil, 1/2 cup soy sauce, 1 medium onion, chopped, 3 tablespoons minced garlic, 2 bunches green onions, chopped and 3 tablespoons chopped fresh cilantro in a bowl and mix well. Use to marinate 4 whole chicken breasts or chicken tenders in the refrigerator for 4 to 12 hours. You can drain the chicken and grill over hot coals or place the chicken and marinade in a large skillet and sauté until the chicken is cooked through.

Chicken Breasts in Tomato Sauce

3 pounds boneless skinless
chicken breasts
3 tablespoons olive oil
1 large onion, chopped
6 garlic cloves, minced

1 (28-ounce) can crushed tomatoes
1 teaspoon basil
1 teaspoon oregano
1 teaspoon rosemary
Salt and pepper to taste

• Brown the chicken in 1 1/2 teaspoons of the olive oil in a large heavy saucepan. Remove the chicken to a platter and keep warm. Add the remaining olive oil, onion and garlic to the saucepan. Sauté until the onion is transparent. Return the chicken to the saucepan. Add the tomatoes. Bring to a boil over medium-high heat and reduce the heat. Add the basil, oregano and rosemary. Simmer, covered, for 30 minutes. Season with salt and pepper to taste. Serve over white rice or pasta, or serve with mashed potatoes and vegetables.

YIELD: 8 SERVINGS

Per Serving (excluding unknown items); 273 Calories; 8 g Fat (25.0% calories from fat); 41 g Protein; 9 g Carbohydrate; 99 mg Cholesterol; 243 mg Sodium. Exchanges: 0 Grain (Starch); 5 1/2 Lean Meat; 1 1/2 Vegetable; 1 Fat.

Chicken Dorito Casserole

1 (10-ounce) can each cream of
mushroom soup and cream of
chicken soup
1 (10-ounce) can tomatoes with
green chiles

1/2 cup finely chopped onion
8 ounces Velveeta cheese, cut into pieces
2 teaspoons cumin
1 chicken, cooked and chopped
1 (10-ounce) package Doritos, crushed

• Combine the soups, tomatoes with green chiles, onion, cheese and cumin in a large saucepan. Cook over low heat until the cheese is melted, stirring constantly. Layer the chicken and Doritos in a 9×13-inch baking dish. Pour the sauce over the layers. Bake at 400 degrees for 25 minutes.

YIELD: 4 TO 6 SERVINGS

Chicken Enchiladas

2 (10-ounce) cans cream of chicken soup

2 (10-ounce) cans tomatoes with green chiles

2 cups sour cream

Salt and pepper to taste

2 pounds boneless skinless chicken breasts, broiled and chopped

1/2 large onion, lightly browned

1 envelope taco seasoning mix

Shredded Monterey Jack cheese to taste

12 to 16 flour tortillas

- Mix the soup, tomatoes with green chiles, sour cream, salt and pepper in a bowl. Spoon a small amount in the bottom of two 11×13-inch glass baking dishes.

- Combine the chicken, onion, taco seasoning mix and cheese in a bowl and mix well.

- Dip each tortilla in the sauce, holding onto the tortilla with both hands. Fill with the chicken mixture and roll up. Arrange in the prepared baking dishes. Each baking dish will hold 6 to 8 roll-ups. Pour the remaining sauce over the top and sprinkle with cheese.

- Bake at 350 degrees for 1 hour or until heated through and the cheese melts.

Note: If baking only 1 dish, bake for 30 minutes. You may prepare ahead and freeze before baking.

YIELD: 6 TO 8 SERVINGS

Enchiladas Verdes

1 large onion, chopped

3 garlic cloves, minced or pressed

3 tablespoons olive oil

1 pound tomatillos, husks removed

1/4 cup chopped fresh cilantro

1 jalapeño chile, seeded and finely chopped

1 teaspoon sugar

1 teaspoon oregano

1 teaspoon basil

1 teaspoon cumin

1 teaspoon salt

12 corn tortillas

1 1/2 cups shredded cooked chicken

2 cups (8 ounces) shredded Monterey Jack cheese or other white Mexican cheese

2 cups (8 ounces) shredded Cheddar cheese

2 cups sour cream

- Sauté the onion and garlic in the olive oil in a skillet until the onion is transparent. Chop the tomatillos and add to the onion mixture. Simmer until soft and thickened, stirring constantly. Add the cilantro, jalapeño chile, sugar, oregano, basil, cumin and salt.

- Oil a large baking dish. Dip the tortillas 1 at a time in the sauce to soften. Fill each tortilla with 1 tablespoon of the chicken, 1 tablespoon of the Monterey Jack cheese and 1 tablespoon of the Cheddar cheese and roll up. Arrange seam side down in the prepared baking dish. Cover with the remaining sauce, remaining Monterey Jack cheese and remaining Cheddar cheese.

- Bake at 350 degrees for 30 minutes or until bubbly. Top with the sour cream.

Note: The traditional method of softening the tortillas is to fry 1 at a time in hot vegetable oil in a skillet for 30 seconds on each side, turning once. Be careful not to overcook since the tortillas should not be hard. This recipe uses the sauce to soften because it reduces the amount of fat.

Yield: 4 to 6 servings

Poppy Seed Chicken

1 whole chicken, or 3 to 4 chicken breasts, cooked

2 cups sour cream

2 (10-ounce) cans cream of chicken soup

Dash of fresh lemon juice

Salt and pepper to taste

$1/2$ cup (1 stick) butter

2 tablespoons poppy seeds

34 to 40 butter crackers, crushed

2 cups wild or white rice, cooked

- Cut the chicken into bite-size pieces, discarding the skin and bones.

- Combine the sour cream, soup, lemon juice, salt and pepper in a bowl and mix well.

- Melt the butter in a skillet. Stir in the poppy seeds and cracker crumbs.

- Layer the rice and chicken pieces in a buttered baking dish. Pour the sour cream mixture over the chicken. Sprinkle with the poppy seed mixture.

- Bake at 350 degrees for 30 minutes.

YIELD: 6 TO 8 SERVINGS

Chicken Potpie

2 tablespoons butter

2 tablespoons flour

1 cup warm chicken broth

Salt, pepper and onion powder to taste

1/4 cup milk

1/2 (10-ounce) can cream of chicken soup

1 (10-ounce) package frozen mixed vegetables

2 cups frozen hash brown potatoes

1 (6-ounce) can sliced mushrooms, drained

1 pound boneless skinless chicken breasts, cooked and chopped

1 prepared pie pastry

1 egg, beaten

- Melt the butter in a saucepan. Whisk in the flour. Cook over low heat until bubbly. Add the warm broth.

- Bring to a boil over medium heat, whisking constantly. Cook for 2 minutes longer, whisking constantly. Remove from the heat.

- Season with salt, pepper and onion powder. Add the milk and soup. Stir in the mixed vegetables, hash brown potatoes, mushrooms and chicken. Add additional milk if the mixture is too thick. Spoon into a 10-cup baking dish.

- Roll the pie pastry into a large circle. Place over the baking dish, sealing and fluting the edge and cutting vents. Brush with the egg.

- Bake at 375 degrees for 30 minutes or until the crust is golden brown.

YIELD: 4 TO 6 SERVINGS

Chicken Wellington

1 package puff pastry	1/2 teaspoon thyme
1 egg	Salt and pepper to taste
1 tablespoon water	2 tablespoons butter
3 ounces cream cheese	3/4 cup sliced mushrooms
1 tablespoon Dijon mustard	1 medium onion, finely chopped
4 boneless skinless chicken breasts	1 tablespoon chopped fresh parsley

- Thaw the puff pastry at room temperature for 30 minutes. Beat the egg with the water in a small bowl. Mix the cream cheese and Dijon mustard in a small bowl. Sprinkle the chicken with the thyme. Season with salt and pepper.

- Heat 1 tablespoon of the butter in a skillet over medium-high heat. Add the chicken. Cook until brown. Remove to a platter. Cover and chill for 15 minutes or up to 24 hours.

- Add the remaining butter to the skillet. Reduce the heat to medium. Add the mushrooms, onion and parsley. Sauté until tender and the liquid is evaporated.

- Unfold the pastry on a lightly floured surface. Roll into a 14-inch square. Cut into four 7-inch squares. Spoon about 1 tablespoon of the mushroom mixture onto each square. Top with the chicken. Spread 1 heaping tablespoon of the cream cheese mixture over the chicken. Brush the edges of the squares with the egg mixture. Fold each corner to the center on top of the chicken and seal the edges. Place seam side down on a baking sheet. (You may freeze and place in sealable plastic bags at this point.) Brush with the egg mixture.

- Bake at 325 degrees for 25 minutes or until golden brown.

Note: If frozen, bake for 1 hour.

YIELD: 4 SERVINGS

King Ranch Chicken

1 medium bell pepper, chopped
1 medium onion, chopped
$^1/_4$ cup ($^1/_2$ stick) margarine
1 (10-ounce) can cream of mushroom soup
1 (10-ounce) can cream of chicken soup
2 (10-ounce) cans tomatoes with green chiles
2 cups chopped cooked chicken
12 corn tortillas, torn into small pieces
2 cups (8 ounces) shredded Cheddar cheese

- Sauté the bell pepper and onion in the margarine in a skillet until tender. Add the soups, tomatoes with green chiles and chicken and mix well.

- Layer the tortillas, chicken mixture and cheese $^1/_3$ at a time in a 9×13-inch baking dish.

- Bake, uncovered, at 325 degrees for 40 minutes or until bubbly.

YIELD: 8 SERVINGS

Homemade Suet for Birds

Combine 1 cup bacon drippings, 1 cup cornmeal, 1 cup water, 1 tablespoon peanut butter and $^1/_2$ cup syrup, jelly or preserves in a saucepan and mix well. Cook until heated through. Remove from the heat to cool. Feed the birds.

Heavenly Chicken Lasagna

1 tablespoon butter or margarine
1/2 onion, chopped
1 (10-ounce) can reduced-fat
cream of chicken soup
1 (10-ounce) container refrigerated
reduced-fat Alfredo sauce
1 (7-ounce) jar chopped pimentos
1 (6-ounce) jar sliced mushrooms,
drained
1/3 cup dry white wine
1/2 teaspoon basil

1 (10-ounce) package frozen chopped
spinach, thawed
1 cup cottage cheese
1 cup ricotta cheese
1/2 cup grated Parmesan cheese
1 egg, lightly beaten
3 cups (12 ounces) shredded sharp
Cheddar cheese
9 lasagna noodles, cooked
2 1/2 cups chopped cooked chicken

- Melt the butter in a large skillet over medium-high heat. Add the onion. Sauté for 5 minutes or until tender. Stir in the soup, Alfredo sauce, undrained pimentos, mushrooms, wine and basil. Remove from the heat. Reserve 1 cup of the sauce.

- Drain the spinach well, pressing between paper towels to absorb the excess moisture. Combine the spinach, cottage cheese, ricotta cheese, Parmesan cheese and egg in a bowl and mix well.

- Reserve 1 cup of the Cheddar cheese. Arrange 3 of the lasagna noodles in a lightly greased 9×13-inch baking pan. Layer the remaining sauce, spinach mixture, chicken, remaining cheese and remaining noodles 1/2 at a time in the prepared pan. Cover with the reserved sauce. (You may cover and chill up to 1 day ahead at this point.)

- Bake at 350 degrees for 45 minutes. Sprinkle with the reserved Cheddar cheese. Bake for 5 minutes or until the cheese melts. Let stand for 10 minutes before serving.

Note: The lasagna may be frozen before baking. Thaw before baking and bake for 5 to 10 minutes longer.

YIELD: 8 TO 10 SERVINGS

Chicken Noodle Casserole

6 chicken pieces	1/2 onion, chopped
12 ounces medium egg noodles	1/2 bell pepper, chopped
2 (10-ounce) cans cream of	Salt and pepper to taste
chicken soup	Shredded mild Cheddar cheese

- Boil the chicken in water to cover in a saucepan until cooked through. Remove the chicken to a platter, reserving the broth in the saucepan. Chop the chicken, discarding the skin and bones. Cook the noodles in the reserved broth in the saucepan until al dente. Drain, reserving 1 cup of the broth.

- Combine the chicken, noodles, soup, onion, bell pepper, salt and pepper in a large bowl and toss to mix well. Add the reserved broth and mix well. Spoon into an oblong baking dish. Cover the top with cheese.

- Bake at 350 degrees until bubbly and the cheese melts.

YIELD: 4 TO 6 SERVINGS

Chicken Bacon Parmesan Penne

12 to 15 slices bacon	1 cup grated Parmesan cheese
3 large boneless skinless chicken	2 1/2 cups whipping cream
breasts, cut into small strips	Salt and pepper to taste
2 garlic cloves, minced	1/2 cup sliced green onions
16 ounces penne, cooked, drained	

- Cook the bacon in a large skillet over medium heat until tender-crisp. Drain the bacon, reserving 2 tablespoons of the drippings in the skillet. Crumble the bacon.

- Sauté the chicken and garlic in the reserved drippings in the skillet until the chicken is cooked through. Stir in the pasta, cheese, whipping cream, salt and pepper. Simmer over medium-low heat until the sauce is thickened, stirring frequently. Stir in the bacon and green onions.

YIELD: 4 SERVINGS

Chicken Parmesan

4 boneless chicken breasts

1 egg, beaten

1/2 cup bread crumbs

1/4 cup olive oil

2 (8-ounce) cans tomato sauce

2 tablespoons Worcestershire sauce

2 tablespoons butter

2 teaspoons basil

1/2 cup grated Parmesan cheese

Sliced provolone or mozzarella cheese

- Pound the chicken breasts to flatten 1/2 inch thick using a meat mallet. Dip each chicken breast in the beaten egg. Coat lightly with the bread crumbs.

- Brown the chicken breasts in the olive oil in a skillet. Arrange in a baking dish.

- Combine the tomato sauce, Worcestershire sauce, butter and basil in a saucepan. Simmer for 20 minutes. Pour over the chicken. Sprinkle with the Parmesan cheese.

- Bake, covered, at 325 degrees for 45 minutes. Uncover and arrange a cheese slice on top of each chicken breast.

- Serve with cooked angel hair pasta tossed with butter and chopped fresh basil.

YIELD: 4 SERVINGS

Chicken Spaghetti

4 chicken breasts

1 garlic clove

1 rib celery

1 small onion, chopped

1/2 cup (1 stick) margarine

12 ounces uncooked thin spaghetti

1 pound Velveeta cheese, cut into cubes

1 (10-ounce) can tomatoes with green chiles

1 (10-ounce) can cream of chicken soup

1 tablespoon Worcestershire sauce

Salt and pepper to taste

- Boil the chicken with the garlic and celery in water to cover in a saucepan until the chicken is cooked through. Drain the chicken, reserving the broth and discarding the garlic and celery. Chop the chicken, discarding the skin and bones.

- Sauté the onion in the margarine in a skillet until translucent. Cook the spaghetti in the reserved broth in a saucepan for 9 minutes.

- Microwave the cheese and tomatoes with green chiles in a microwave-safe dish on High until smooth.

- Combine the cheese mixture, soup, undrained sautéed onion, Worcestershire sauce and chicken in a large bowl and mix well. Season with salt and pepper. Add the hot spaghetti a small amount at a time, mixing well after each addition. Spoon into a greased 9×13-inch baking dish.

- Bake at 350 degrees for 45 minutes or until bubbly.

YIELD: 4 TO 6 SERVINGS

Chicken Tetrazzini

2 cups Mornay Sauce (below)

2 cups medium cream sauce

6 cups drained cooked spaghetti

4 cups coarsely chopped cooked chicken, turkey or shrimp

1/2 cup mushrooms, sautéed

1/4 cup dry sherry

Freshly grated Parmesan cheese

Paprika

- Combine the Mornay Sauce, cream sauce, spaghetti, chicken, mushrooms and sherry in a large bowl and toss to mix well. Spoon into a well-buttered shallow baking dish. Cover generously with cheese. Sprinkle lightly with paprika.

- Bake at 350 degrees until brown and bubbly.

Note: You may use toasted almonds instead of the mushrooms.

YIELD: 8 SERVINGS

Mornay Sauce

1/2 cup (1 stick) butter

1 cup flour

4 cups milk

2 pounds Velveeta cheese, cut into cubes

1 can beer

- Melt the butter in a saucepan. Add the flour. Cook until blended, stirring constantly. Stir in the milk. Cook until smooth, stirring constantly. Boil for 1 minute. Remove from the heat.

- Add the cheese. Beat at medium speed for 15 minutes or longer. The sauce improves with the amount of beating. Add the beer a small amount at a time until the sauce is the desired consistency, beating constantly.

Note: You may make the sauce and store in the refrigerator for several days.
Beat again before using to restore its light consistency.

Sherry Dove Casserole

15 to 20 dove breasts
1¹/2 cups flour
¹/4 cup vegetable oil
2 bunches green onions with tops, chopped
2 bell peppers, chopped
4 tomatoes, chopped
2 hot red peppers, chopped
4 garlic cloves, chopped
¹/2 cup (1 stick) butter
4 (10-ounce) cans chicken broth
4 teaspoons (heaping) Tony Chachere's Creole seasoning
1 tablespoon (heaping) Cavender's
1 cup red wine
1 cup white sherry

- Roll the doves in the flour to coat. Fry in the hot oil in a skillet until light brown. Sauté the green onions, bell peppers, tomatoes, hot red peppers and garlic in the butter in a skillet for 10 minutes. Add the broth, Creole seasoning, Cavender's and doves and mix well. Simmer for 30 minutes. Add the wine and sherry. Simmer for 30 minutes. Serve over hot cooked rice.

YIELD: 15 TO 20 DOVE BREASTS

Doves Southern Style

12 doves or quail
Flour for dusting
2 tablespoons butter
2 tablespoons vegetable oil
2 (10-ounce) cans chicken stock
2 garlic cloves, minced
2 tablespoons finely chopped jalapeño chiles
1 onion, chopped
2 tomatoes, chopped
¹/2 cup white wine
8 ounces fresh mushrooms

- Dust the birds with flour. Brown in the butter and oil in a Dutch oven. Add the stock, garlic, jalapeño chiles and onion. Bake at 325 degrees for 1¹/2 hours. Remove from the oven. Add the tomatoes, wine and mushrooms. Simmer on the top of the stove until heated through and the gravy is a medium-thick consistency. Serve over wild rice.

YIELD: 6 SERVINGS

Party Ducks

2 apples

Ribs of celery

4 ducks

2 (10-ounce) cans consommé

1 can water

1 1/2 cups (3 sticks) butter

2/3 cup sherry

1/2 cup bourbon

1 (5-ounce) jar currant jelly

1/4 cup Worcestershire sauce

- Cut the apples into halves. Cut the celery into pieces. Stuff the ducks with the apples and celery. Mix the consommé and water in a large baking dish. Arrange the ducks breast side down in the mixture.

- Bake, tightly covered, at 350 degrees for 3 hours or until the ducks are very tender. Remove from the oven.

- Heat the butter, sherry, bourbon, jelly and Worcestershire sauce in a small saucepan over low heat until smooth. (You may thicken with a little flour or cornstarch if the sauce is too thin.)

- Cut the breast portion from the ducks, discarding the remaining portions. Arrange in a greased shallow baking dish. Pour the sauce over the duck breasts.

- Bake, covered, at 350 degrees until heated through. Serve on a mound of rice sprinkled with crumbled crisp-cooked bacon with the sauce on the side.

YIELD: 6 TO 8 SERVINGS

Governor Huckabee's Favorite Duck

8 duck breasts
1 (8-ounce) bottle Italian salad dressing
16 slices bacon

- Rinse the duck breasts thoroughly. Place in a sealable plastic bag. Pour the salad dressing over the duck breasts and seal the bag.

- Marinate in the refrigerator for 8 to 12 hours, turning every 2 hours.

- Drain the duck breasts, discarding the marinade. Wrap each duck breast in 2 slices of bacon, securing with wooden picks if necessary. Place on a grill rack.

- Grill for 15 minutes and turn. Grill for 12 minutes or until the bacon and duck breasts are cooked through.

YIELD: 8 SERVINGS

"While most people are comfortably slumbering in bed on a cold winter morning, I am making my way through a narrow ditch of water in the woods in a johnboat powered by an undersized motor and full of oversized men clad in camo and accompanied by a black Labrador retriever who can't contain his excitement. While those other folks have their eyes closed shut under thick blankets, my friends and I are wide-eyed at a still dark sky waiting for a glimpse or sound of what has brought us to the woods—a mallard duck. About the time the alarm clocks are ringing in some bedrooms, we will hopefully have started the celebration of completing another successful duck hunt in the green timber woods of Arkansas. It's for that experience we do more than get up early. We never even went to sleep the night before!"
—The Governor
Mike Huckabee

Duck and Wild Rice Casserole

This recipe is so delicious that its fame is widespread. Certainly no collection of Pine Bluff's favorite recipes would be complete without it.

2 medium ducks (3 cups chopped cooked duck)

3 ribs celery

1 onion, cut into halves

Salt and pepper to taste

1 (4-ounce) can sliced mushrooms

1/2 cup chopped onion

1/2 cup (1 stick) margarine

1/4 cup flour

1 1/2 cups half-and-half

1 tablespoon chopped fresh parsley

1 (6-ounce) package seasoned wild and long grain rice, cooked

1 1/2 teaspoons salt

1/4 teaspoon pepper

Slivered almonds

- Combine the ducks, celery and onion in a large saucepan. Season with salt and pepper to taste. Add enough water to cover. Boil for 1 hour or until the ducks are tender. Drain the ducks, reserving the broth. Chop the duck, discarding the skin and bones.

- Drain the mushrooms, reserving the liquid. Add enough of the reserved duck broth to the reserved mushroom liquid to measure 1 1/2 cups. Sauté the onion in the margarine in a skillet until translucent. Stir in the flour. Add the mushrooms and broth mixture and mix well. Add the half-and-half, parsley and rice and mix well. Season with 1 1/2 teaspoons salt and 1/4 teaspoon pepper. Spoon into a greased 2-quart baking dish. Sprinkle with the almonds.

- Bake, covered, at 350 degrees for 15 to 20 minutes. Bake, uncovered, for 5 to 10 minutes longer.

Note: If you don't have ducks, try substituting chicken—it's still good.

YIELD: 6 SERVINGS

Smothered Quail

1 medium onion, finely chopped

8 ounces fresh mushrooms, sliced

3 tablespoons butter

8 to 12 quail breasts

3 tablespoons butter

1 tablespoon vegetable oil

1/2 cup dry white wine or vermouth

1 (10-ounce) can cream of mushroom soup

1 cup light cream or half-and-half

- Sauté the onion and mushrooms in 3 tablespoons butter in a skillet until tender. Remove from the skillet.

- Sauté the birds in 3 tablespoons butter and 1 tablespoon oil in a skillet until brown. Remove from the skillet. Drain the excess drippings from the skillet. Add the wine, stirring to deglaze the skillet. Add the soup, sautéed onion mixture and cream and mix well. Return the birds to the skillet and spoon the sauce over the top.

- Simmer, covered, for 30 minutes.

Note: You may substitute chicken breasts for the quail.

YIELD: 8 SERVINGS

Quail or Dove on Toast

20 whole quail or dove breasts

1 (8-ounce) bottle Italian salad dressing

Salt and pepper to taste

1/2 cup (1 stick) butter

1/2 cup water, wine or chicken broth

3 tablespoons Worcestershire sauce

2 tablespoons water, wine or chicken broth

Toasted bread or grits

- Place the birds in a large sealable plastic bag. Pour the salad dressing over the birds and seal the bag. Marinate in the refrigerator for 24 hours or longer, turning the bag occasionally. Season with salt and pepper to taste.

- Drain the birds, discarding the marinade. Cook the birds in the butter in a 10-inch skillet over medium-high heat for 15 minutes or until brown. (Do not overcrowd the birds. Use multiple skillets if needed, just be sure to use the same amount of butter, water and Worcestershire sauce per skillet.) Add 1/2 cup water. Reduce the heat to low. Steam, covered, for 30 minutes. Add the Worcestershire sauce. Steam for 15 minutes. Remove the birds to a hot platter.

- Add 2 tablespoons water to the skillet, stirring to deglaze the skillet. If the sauce is too thin, increase the heat. Boil for 1 minute or until the desired consistency. Pour into a serving bowl. Arrange the birds over the toasted bread or grits. Spoon the sauce over the top.

YIELD: 4 SERVINGS

Shake'n Bake Quail

8 quail

1 cup Italian salad dressing

Shake'n Bake for chicken

Lemon pepper to taste

- Place the birds in a sealable plastic bag. Add the salad dressing and seal the bag. Marinate in the refrigerator for 8 to 12 hours. Drain the birds, discarding the marinade. Coat with Shake'n Bake. Arrange on a baking sheet. Season with lemon pepper. Bake at 350 degrees for 30 to 40 minutes or until cooked through.

YIELD: 2 SERVINGS

Creole Catfish with Mushroom Crawfish Sauce

2 tablespoons Creole seasoning
8 catfish fillets
1/4 cup mayonnaise
1 cup fresh mushrooms, sliced
1/2 cup sliced shallots or
green onions
1/4 cup minced fresh parsley
2 tablespoons crushed garlic

8 ounces peeled crawfish tails, drained
2 tablespoons butter
2 (10-ounce) cans cream of
mushroom soup
2 tablespoons sherry
Salt, white pepper, black pepper and
cayenne pepper to taste
2 tablespoons butter

• Rub the Creole seasoning on each side of the fish. Spread each side with a thin layer of mayonnaise. Let stand for 15 minutes. Sauté the mushrooms, shallots, parsley, garlic and crawfish tails in 2 tablespoons butter in a skillet for 3 to 5 minutes. Add the soup and sherry and mix until smooth. Season with the salt, white pepper, black pepper and cayenne pepper.

• Cook the fish in 2 tablespoons butter in a skillet over high heat for 3 minutes per side. Arrange in a baking dish. Pour the sauce over the fish. Bake at 350 degrees for 20 minutes. Serve over angel hair pasta or fettuccini.

YIELD: 8 SERVINGS

Pecan Catfish

6 tablespoons Dijon mustard
1/4 cup milk

1 cup ground pecans
4 catfish fillets

• Mix the Dijon mustard and milk in a shallow dish. Spread the pecans in a separate shallow dish or on a piece of waxed paper. Dip the fish in the mustard mixture to cover lightly. Roll in the pecans to coat, shaking off the excess. Arrange on a greased baking sheet.

• Bake at 450 degrees for 10 to 12 minutes or until the fish flakes easily.

YIELD: 4 SERVINGS

Salmon with Sun-Dried Tomato Sauce

2 teaspoons olive oil

2 tablespoons minced shallots

1 tablespoon strained lemon juice

1/2 cup dry white wine

6 sun-dried tomatoes, rehydrated and minced

1/2 teaspoon coarse salt

1/2 teaspoon fresh ground pepper

1 tablespoon fresh basil, minced

1 tablespoon fresh thyme, minced

2 teaspoons fresh rosemary leaves, minced

1/2 cup dry bread crumbs

2 (12-ounce) salmon fillets, skinned

2 teaspoons olive oil

- Heat 2 teaspoons olive oil in a 10-inch skillet over medium heat. Add the shallots. Sauté for 1 minute or until light golden brown. Add the lemon juice, wine and sun-dried tomatoes. Increase the heat to medium-high. Cook for 2 minutes or until the sauce is reduced to 1/2 cup. Season with salt and pepper. (The sauce can be made up to 1 hour before cooking the fish. Reheat over low heat, just before removing the fish from the oven.)

- Mix the basil, thyme, rosemary and bread crumbs on a piece of waxed paper. Dredge the fish in the bread crumb mixture to coat. Arrange 2 inches apart in a 9×13-inch baking dish sprayed with nonstick cooking spray. Drizzle with 2 teaspoons olive oil.

- Bake at 400 degrees for 8 to 10 minutes or until the fish is opaque and barely flakes easily. Remove to a serving platter. Cut each fillet into halves crosswise. Spoon the sauce over the top.

YIELD: 2 SERVINGS

Per Serving (excluding unknown items): 649 Calories; 22 g Fat (33.8% calories from fat); 73 g Protein; 27g Carbohydrate; 177 mg Cholesterol; 1061 mg Sodium. Exchanges: 1 1/2 Grain (Starch); 9 1/2 Lean Meat; 1/2 Vegetable; 0 Fruit; 2 Fat.

Grilled Marinated Tuna Steaks

¹/4 cup vegetable oil	2 teaspoons sesame oil
¹/4 cup lime juice	2 teaspoons honey
1 tablespoon water	4 fresh tuna steaks, 1 inch thick
1 tablespoon soy sauce	

• Combine the vegetable oil, lime juice, water, soy sauce, sesame oil and honey in a bowl and mix well. Place the fish in a sealable plastic bag. Pour the marinade over the fish and seal the bag. Marinate in the refrigerator for 6 hours, turning the bag occasionally. Drain the fish, discarding the marinade. Place the fish on a grill rack. Grill over medium-hot coals for 8 to 12 minutes or until the fish flakes easily.

YIELD: 4 SERVINGS

Cajun Creation

1 pound sausage, sliced	2 garlic cloves, minced
1 cup chopped green bell pepper	1 cup uncooked rice
1 cup chopped celery	2 cups water
1 cup chopped onion	1 (14-ounce) can tomatoes
¹/2 cup chopped green onions	1 pound crawfish tails
2 tablespoons butter	2 teaspoons (or more) Creole seasoning

• Sauté the sausage, bell pepper, celery, onion and green onions in the butter in a large skillet or Dutch oven until tender but not brown. Stir in the garlic, rice, water, tomatoes, crawfish tails and Creole seasoning. Bring to a boil, stirring once or twice. Reduce the heat. Simmer, covered for 20 minutes or until the rice is tender. The mixture should be slightly moist. Adjust the seasoning to taste.

Note: You may substitute shrimp or chicken for the crawfish tails. If you don't like whole tomato pieces, you may process the tomatoes in a blender until smooth.

YIELD: 10 SERVINGS

Creole Country Crawfish Casserole

3 ounces cream cheese

1 (10-ounce) can golden mushroom soup

1 teaspoon Tabasco sauce, or to taste

Red pepper to taste

3 cups cooked rice

1 cup frozen green peas

1/4 cup pimentos

2 cups crawfish tails, or 2 (1-pound) packages crawfish tails, drained

Fresh mushrooms to taste, or 1 (8-ounce) can mushrooms, drained

1 cup chopped celery

1 cup chopped onion

2 tablespoons minced garlic

2 tablespoons butter

1 cup (4 ounces) shredded Cheddar cheese

- Melt the cream cheese in a saucepan. Combine with the soup, Tabasco sauce and red pepper in a large bowl and mix well. Stir in the rice, peas, pimentos and crawfish tails.

- Sauté the mushrooms, celery, onion and garlic in the butter in a skillet until the onion is translucent. Stir into the rice mixture. Spoon into a 9×13-inch baking dish.

- Bake, covered, at 350 degrees for 25 to 30 minutes or until cooked through. Uncover and sprinkle with the cheese. Bake until the cheese melts.

Note: You may substitute shrimp for the crawfish tails.

YIELD: 6 TO 8 SERVINGS

Crawfish Fettuccini

3 medium onions, chopped

2 medium bell peppers, chopped

1 1/2 cups (3 sticks) margarine

1/4 cup flour

1/4 cup parsley flakes

3 pounds shelled crawfish tails

2 cups half-and-half

1 pound Velveeta cheese, cut into cubes

2 teaspoons jalapeño relish

3 tablespoons minced garlic

Salt, red pepper and black pepper to taste

16 ounces fettuccini, cooked

Grated Parmesan cheese

- Sauté the onions and bell peppers in the margarine in a skillet until tender. Add the flour. Cook for 10 minutes, stirring frequently to prevent sticking. Add the parsley and crawfish tails. Cook, covered, for 15 minutes. Add the half-and-half, Velveeta cheese, relish, garlic, salt, red pepper and black pepper and mix well. Cook, covered, for 15 minutes. Remove from the heat.

- Combine the crawfish mixture and pasta in a large bowl and toss to mix well. Spoon into a 4-quart baking dish.

- Bake at 350 degrees for 15 to 20 minutes or until bubbly. Sprinkle with cheese.

Note: You may substitute 3 pounds shrimp, peeled and chopped, for the crawfish.

YIELD: 12 TO 15 SERVINGS

Jambalaya

1/4 cup (1/2 stick) margarine	1 1/2 cups chopped onions
6 ounces smoked ham (such as Cure 81), chopped (about 1 1/2 cups)	1 1/2 cups chopped celery
	1 cup chopped green bell peppers
6 ounces andouille smoked sausage (or any smoked sausage or kielbasa), chopped (about 1 cup)	Seasoning Mix (below)
	1/2 teaspoon minced garlic
	2 cups uncooked rice
6 ounces chopped cooked chicken (about 1 cup) (optional)	4 cups beef, pork or chicken stock
	6 ounces small shrimp (about 1 cup)

• Melt the margarine in a large cast-iron skillet over high heat. Add the ham, sausage and chicken. Cook for 5 minutes, stirring occasionally. Add the onions, celery, bell peppers, Seasoning Mix and garlic and mix well. Continue to cook for 10 to 12 minutes or until brown, stirring to deglaze the skillet occasionally. Stir in the rice.

• Cook for 5 minutes, stirring to deglaze the skillet occasionally. Add the stock and shrimp and mix well. Bring to a boil and reduce the heat. Simmer for 20 minutes or until the rice is tender but still a bit crunchy, stirring occasionally toward the end of the cooking time. Discard the bay leaves. Serve immediately.

YIELD: 4 (2-CUP) SERVINGS

Seasoning Mix

4 small whole bay leaves	1 teaspoon cayenne pepper or ground red pepper
1 teaspoon salt	
1 teaspoon white pepper	1/2 teaspoon cumin
1 teaspoon dry mustard	1/2 teaspoon black pepper
1 teaspoon gumbo filé (optional)	1/2 teaspoon thyme

• Combine the bay leaves, salt, white pepper, dry mustard, gumbo filé, cayenne pepper, cumin, black pepper and thyme in a small bowl and mix well.

Shrimp Bienville

1 cup finely chopped yellow onion

1 cup chopped green onions

^{1}/2 cup (1 stick) butter

6 ounces fresh mushrooms, chopped

^{1}/3 cup flour

2 cups chicken consommé

1 cup dry white wine

1^1/2 cups uncooked shrimp, peeled

4 egg yolks, lightly beaten

^{1}/4 cup whipping cream

2 tablespoons lemon juice

^{1}/4 teaspoon white pepper

^{1}/8 teaspoon cayenne pepper

• Sauté the yellow onion and green onions in the butter in a skillet for 10 minutes or until wilted. Add the mushrooms. Simmer for 20 to 30 minutes. Remove from the heat. Sprinkle with the flour. Return to medium heat and mix well. Add the consommé and wine gradually, stirring constantly. Stir in the shrimp. Cook for 10 to 15 minutes or until thickened, stirring constantly. Remove from the heat. Beat the egg yolks with the whipping cream in a bowl. Add some of the hot mixture to the egg yolk mixture. Stir the egg yolk mixture into the hot mixture. Add the lemon juice, white pepper and cayenne pepper. Serve over rice.

YIELD: 4 TO 6 SERVINGS

Shrimp Scampi

^{1}/2 cup (1 stick) butter

1 garlic clove, minced

1 teaspoon olive oil

Tabasco sauce to taste

1 teaspoon each salt and pepper

8 ounces shrimp, peeled and deveined

• Melt the butter over low heat in a large heavy skillet. Add the garlic. Sauté for 2 minutes. Add the olive oil, Tabasco sauce, salt and pepper. Increase the heat to medium. Add the shrimp. Cook for 5 to 15 minutes or until the shrimp turn pink. Serve over angel hair pasta.

Note: You may marinate the shrimp in the sauce in a glass dish for 8 to 12 hours. Drain and grill for 5 minutes or until the shrimp turn pink.

YIELD: 4 SERVINGS

Coconut Shrimp

1/2 cup flour

1 teaspoon dry mustard

1 teaspoon salt

2 eggs

1 cup cream of coconut

1 cup flaked coconut

2/3 cup bread crumbs or cracker crumbs

1 pound peeled large shrimp with tails

Vegetable oil for deep-frying

Tropical Dipping Sauce (below)

- Combine the flour, dry mustard and salt in a bowl and mix well. Beat the eggs in a mixing bowl until frothy. Add the cream of coconut and mix well. Mix the flaked coconut and bread crumbs in a bowl. Coat the shrimp with the flour mixture. Dip in the egg mixture. Coat with the coconut mixture. Arrange the shrimp on a baking sheet. Chill until just before serving time.

- Heat the oil in a deep fryer to 375 degrees. Add the shrimp. Deep-fry for 1 to 2 minutes or until light golden brown. Drain on paper towels. Serve with Tropical Dipping Sauce.

YIELD: 4 TO 6 SERVINGS

Tropical Dipping Sauce

1 (8-ounce) can cream of coconut

1 (8-ounce) can crushed pineapple

- Combine the cream of coconut and pineapple in a bowl and mix well. Store, covered, in the refrigerator.

Note: You may want to prepare only as much sauce as you need because this makes a lot of sauce.

Poblano Shrimp Enchiladas

12 ounces unpeeled medium fresh shrimp

2 tablespoons olive oil

1 large poblano chile, cut into halves and seeded

1 onion, chopped

1 tomato, chopped

1/4 teaspoon salt

1/2 teaspoon oregano

1/4 teaspoon cumin

1/4 teaspoon pepper

3 tablespoons olive oil

1/2 cup sour cream

8 corn tortillas

1 (10-ounce) can green enchilada sauce

1 1/2 cups (6 ounces) shredded Monterey Jack cheese

- Peel the shrimp and devein. Chop the shrimp coarsely. Brush a 7×11-inch baking dish with 2 tablespoons olive oil.

- Place the chile on a baking sheet. Bake at 450 degrees for 3 minutes or until blistered and dark. Enclose in a paper bag. Let stand for 10 minutes. Peel the chile and remove the seeds. Chop the chile.

- Sauté the chile, onion, tomato, salt, oregano, cumin and pepper in 3 tablespoons olive oil in a skillet for 4 minutes. Add the shrimp. Sauté for 1 minute. Remove from the heat to cool for 5 minutes. Stir in the sour cream.

- Heat the tortillas using the package directions. Spoon the shrimp mixture evenly down the center of each tortilla and roll up. Arrange seam side down in the prepared pan. Top with the enchilada sauce. Sprinkle with the cheese. Chill, covered, for up to 1 day ahead.

- Bake at 350 degrees for 25 minutes or until heated through.

YIELD: 4 SERVINGS

Dijon Cream Sauce

1 red onion, thinly sliced

1/4 cup (1/2 stick) butter

1 to 2 tablespoons Dijon mustard

1 to 2 teaspoons Old Bay seasoning

1/4 cup mayonnaise

4 cups (1 quart) heavy whipping cream

2 tablespoons water

1 tablespoon cornstarch

1 to 2 tablespoons honey

- Cook the onion in the butter in a skillet over medium heat for 15 to 20 minutes or until the onion is caramelized. Mix the Dijon mustard, Old Bay seasoning and mayonnaise in a small bowl. Stir into the onion mixture. Add the cream.

- Bring to a boil over medium heat. Stir in a mixture of the water and cornstarch. Cook over medium-low heat until thickened, stirring constantly. Stir in the honey.

- Serve over fish or crab cakes.

YIELD: 10 TO 12 SERVINGS

Rémoulade Blanc

1 cup mayonnaise

2 tablespoons Creole mustard

4 green onions, finely chopped

2 teaspoons finely chopped parsley

1 tablespoon horseradish

Juice of 1/2 lemon

1 ounce white wine

Pinch of white pepper

Pinch of cayenne pepper

- Whisk the mayonnaise, Creole mustard, green onions, parsley, horseradish, lemon juice, wine, white pepper and cayenne pepper in a bowl until smooth.

- Chill, covered, until ready to serve. Serve with shrimp.

YIELD: 1 3/4 CUPS

Meats

The Old Firehouse Mural—Chiefs George Alford and Ray Jacks

The City of Pine Bluff started its unique beginning as a small trading post high atop a bluff covered in towering pines overlooking the Arkansas River. Since that time, Pine Bluff has grown to include many attractions that make it a magnet for tourists, such as the Arkansas Entertainers Hall of Fame, the Band, Historical and Railroad Museums, the Arts and Science Center for Southeast Arkansas, and the Delta Rivers Nature Center. A visitor can see that Pine Bluff is rich in heritage and arts.

Beef Tenderloin with Port Balsamic Sauce

This sauce will elevate any boring steak to a gourmet dinner.

1 cup ruby port

1 cup dry white wine

2 (8-ounce) beef tenderloin steaks (about 1 1/2 inches thick)

Salt and pepper to taste

Flour for coating

1 tablespoon unsalted butter

1 tablespoon olive oil

1 tablespoon unsalted butter

2 tablespoons balsamic vinegar

2 tablespoons unsalted butter

2 tablespoons heavy cream

- Boil the port and white wine in a small heavy saucepan for 8 minutes or until the mixture is reduced to 2/3 cup.

- Sprinkle the beef with salt and pepper. Dredge in the flour and shake off the excess. Melt 1 tablespoon butter with the olive oil in a large heavy skillet over medium-high heat. Add the beef. Cook for 4 minutes for medium-rare or to the desired degree of doneness. Remove the beef to a platter and tent with foil. (The beef will continue to cook while tented with foil to about medium.)

- Melt 1 tablespoon butter in the skillet. Add the wine mixture and balsamic vinegar. Bring to a boil, stirring to deglaze the skillet. Boil for 2 minutes or until the mixture is reduced to a sauce consistency. Remove from the heat. Add 2 tablespoons butter and whisk until smooth. Stir in the cream. Season with salt and pepper. Serve over the beef.

Note: You may substitute cabernet or merlot for the port.

YIELD: 2 SERVINGS

Herb-Crusted Beef Tenderloin

1/2 cup bread crumbs
1/3 cup chopped fresh basil
3 tablespoons olive oil
1 tablespoon pepper
1 teaspoon salt
3 tablespoons fresh thyme
1 1/2 pounds beef tenderloin
1 tablespoon chopped fresh parsley

- Mix the bread crumbs, basil, olive oil, pepper, salt and thyme in a bowl.

- Moisten the beef with water. Press the crumb mixture over the beef. Arrange the beef on a rack in a roasting pan.

- Bake at 425 degrees for 25 minutes or until a meat thermometer inserted into the thickest portion registers 160 degrees. Sprinkle with the parsley.

Note: This was served at Charity Ball 1999.

YIELD: 3 TO 4 SERVINGS

Texas Beef Brisket

4 pounds beef brisket, trimmed

$1/2$ cup reduced-sodium soy sauce

$1/2$ cup Worcestershire sauce

1 teaspoon garlic powder

1 teaspoon pepper

1 teaspoon seasoned salt

1 onion, sliced

- Place the beef in a roasting pan. Combine the soy sauce, Worcestershire sauce, garlic powder, pepper and seasoned salt in a bowl and mix well. Pour over the brisket, turning to coat.

- Marinate, covered, in the refrigerator for 8 to 12 hours, turning occasionally. Arrange the onion slices on top of the brisket.

- Bake at 250 degrees for 4 to 5 hours. Cut into slices against the grain to serve. Serve with the pan drippings.

YIELD: 6 SERVINGS

Dijon Wine Marinated Rib Roast

1 (3- to 4-pound) boneless rib-eye roast, rib roast or rump roast

1/2 cup burgundy or other dry red wine

2 tablespoons olive oil

2 tablespoons freshly ground pepper

1 tablespoon Dijon mustard

1/2 teaspoon salt

1/8 teaspoon tarragon

1 garlic clove, crushed

- Place the beef in a large sealable plastic bag. Mix the wine, olive oil, pepper, Dijon mustard, salt, tarragon and garlic in a bowl. Pour over the beef and seal the bag. Marinate in the refrigerator for 8 hours, turning the bag occasionally.

- Drain the beef, discarding the marinade. Place the beef on a rack in a shallow roasting pan. Insert a meat thermometer into the thickest portion, making sure not to touch fat or bone.

- Bake at 350 degrees for 1 1/4 hours or until the meat thermometer registers 145 degrees for medium-rare or 160 degrees for medium. Let stand for 10 minutes before slicing.

YIELD: 8 TO 10 SERVINGS

Citrus Marinated Flank Steak

1 (1¹/4- to 1¹/2-pound) flank steak, trimmed
¹/2 cup vegetable oil
¹/4 cup lemon juice
¹/4 to ¹/2 cup chopped fresh parsley
2 garlic cloves, minced
1 teaspoon salt
Pepper to taste

- Place the beef in a sealable plastic bag. Combine the oil, lemon juice, parsley, garlic, salt and pepper in a bowl and mix well. Pour over the beef and seal the bag. Marinate in the refrigerator for 8 to 12 hours.

- Drain the beef, discarding the marinade. Arrange the beef on a grill rack.

- Grill for 6 minutes on each side or to the desired degree of doneness. Cut cross-grain at a 45-degree angle to serve.

YIELD: 4 SERVINGS

Davis Hospital

In 1893, the Hospital and Benevolent Association was organized to raise funds for construction of a hospital for the community. Named after Major W. H. Davis, a major contributor to the Association, the Davis Hospital was completed in July 1910. Located at 11th and Cherry Streets, this new hospital provided needed medical facilities to Pine Bluff. Davis Hospital was the first public owned hospital in Pine Bluff. It continued to be the primary medical facility in Pine Bluff and Jefferson County until September of 1960 when the new Jefferson Hospital was completed. The Jefferson Regional Medical Center as it is now known, was a joint venture by the Pine Bluff and Jefferson County Governments, and has become a regional medical center for Southeast Arkansas.

Skillet Beef Burgundy

1 1/2 pounds lean boneless sirloin steak

2 cups sliced carrots (1/2 inch thick)

2 cups quartered mushrooms

3/4 cup coarsely chopped onion

1 pound small red potatoes, peeled and quartered

1 teaspoon thyme

1/4 teaspoon pepper

1 (10-ounce) can beef consommé

3/4 cup burgundy or other dry red wine

3 tablespoons flour

- Trim the beef and cut into 1-inch cubes. Coat a large nonstick skillet with nonstick cooking spray. Heat over medium-high heat until hot. Add the beef. Cook for 4 minutes or until the beef looses its pink color. Remove the beef from the skillet.

- Drain the skillet. Coat with nonstick cooking spray. Heat over medium-high heat until hot. Add the carrots, mushrooms, onion and potatoes. Sauté for 5 minutes. Return the beef to the skillet. Add the thyme, pepper and consommé and mix well. Cover and reduce the heat. Simmer for 30 minutes or until the beef and vegetables are tender.

- Whisk the wine gradually into the flour in a bowl. Add to the beef mixture. Cook for 5 minutes or until thickened and bubbly, stirring constantly.

YIELD: 5 SERVINGS

Mexican Pepper Steak

$2^{1}/_{2}$ pounds sirloin steaks, cut into $1^{1}/_{2}$-inch strips

1 bell pepper, cut into $1^{1}/_{2}$-inch strips

$^{1}/_{4}$ cup soy sauce

$^{1}/_{4}$ teaspoon cayenne pepper

2 teaspoons garlic powder

$^{1}/_{4}$ teaspoon black pepper

$^{1}/_{2}$ teaspoon salt

$^{1}/_{4}$ teaspoon chili powder

$^{1}/_{8}$ teaspoon cumin

1 (28-ounce) can whole peeled tomatoes, chopped

1 (10-ounce) can tomatoes with green chiles

- Combine the beef, bell pepper, soy sauce, cayenne pepper, garlic powder, black pepper, salt, chili powder and cumin in a large saucepan. Bring to a boil over medium heat and reduce the heat. Simmer for 20 to 30 minutes. Add the tomatoes and tomatoes with green chiles.

- Simmer for 20 minutes over low heat. Serve over rice.

YIELD: 6 SERVINGS

Ground Beef and Green Chile Casserole

1 1/2 pounds ground beef

1/2 onion, chopped

1 tablespoon cumin

1 tablespoon chili powder

1/2 teaspoon salt

1/2 teaspoon garlic powder

1 (10-ounce) can cream of chicken soup

1 (4-ounce) can chopped green chiles

1/2 (13.5 ounce) package Tostitos, crushed

2 cups (8 ounces) shredded Cheddar cheese

- Brown the ground beef and onion in a skillet, stirring until the ground beef is crumbly; drain. Add the cumin, chili powder, salt, garlic powder, soup and green chiles and mix well.

- Layer the Tostitos and ground beef mixture 1/2 at a time in a baking dish sprayed with nonstick cooking spray. Cover the top with the cheese.

- Bake at 350 degrees for 15 minutes or until the cheese melts.

Note: You may top with salsa, sour cream, lettuce and tomatoes.

YIELD: 4 TO 6 SERVINGS

Cheesy Ground Beef Casserole

2 pounds ground round steak

1 teaspoon garlic salt

2 teaspoons salt

2 teaspoons sugar

Pepper to taste

4 (8-ounce) cans tomato sauce

8 ounces cream cheese, softened

2 cups sour cream

5 green onions with tops, thinly sliced

12 ounces medium noodles, cooked and drained

2 cups (8 ounces) shredded Cheddar cheese

- Brown the ground round in a skillet, stirring until crumbly; drain. Add the garlic salt, salt, sugar and pepper. Cook until well blended. Stir in the tomato sauce. Simmer for 15 minutes.

- Combine the cream cheese, sour cream and green onions in a bowl and mix well.

- Layer the noodles, ground round mixture, cream cheese mixture and Cheddar cheese in the order listed $1/2$ at a time in a buttered 4-quart baking dish. (You may prepare up to 24 hours in advance up to this point. Store, covered, in the refrigerator until ready to bake.)

- Bake at 350 degrees for 30 minutes.

YIELD: 8 SERVINGS

Hot Tamale Meatballs

$^1/3$ cup tomato juice

$^3/4$ cup cornmeal

1 tablespoon each cumin and chili powder

$^1/4$ teaspoon salt

2 garlic cloves, minced

$^1/4$ to $^1/2$ teaspoon cayenne pepper

8 ounces ground beef

8 ounces bulk pork sausage

$3^2/3$ cups tomato juice

1 tablespoon each cumin and chili powder

$^1/2$ teaspoon salt

- Combine $^1/3$ cup tomato juice, cornmeal, 1 tablespoon cumin, 1 tablespoon chili powder, $^1/4$ teaspoon salt, garlic and cayenne pepper in a large bowl and mix well. Add the ground beef and sausage and mix well. Shape into $1^1/4$-inch balls.

- Combine $3^2/3$ cups tomato juice, 1 tablespoon cumin, 1 tablespoon chili powder and $^1/2$ teaspoon salt in a Dutch oven and mix well. Bring to a boil. Add the meatballs.

- Simmer, covered, for 45 minutes or until the meatballs are cooked through. Serve over hot cooked rice or pasta.

YIELD: 4 SERVINGS

Beef Ravioli with Pesto Sauce

1 cup whipping cream

1 (3-ounce) jar capers, drained

1 (2-ounce) jar pesto sauce

2 (9-ounce) packages refrigerated beef- or cheese-filled ravioli

2 tablespoons pine nuts, toasted

- Combine the cream, capers and pesto sauce in a large bowl and mix well.

- Cook the pasta using the package directions; drain. Add to the pesto mixture and toss to mix well. Sprinkle with the pine nuts.

- Serve immediately.

Note: You may substitute the homemade Pesto Sauce at right for the commercial pesto.

YIELD: 6 SERVINGS

Pesto Sauce

Process $1^{1}/_{2}$ cups extra-virgin or pure olive oil, 5 large garlic cloves, coarsely chopped, 3 tablespoons pine nuts or chopped walnuts, $1^{1}/_{4}$ teaspoons salt and $^{3}/_{4}$ teaspoon pepper in a blender for 1 minute. Add 2 cups tightly packed fresh basil leaves and 1 cup tightly packed fresh flat-leaf Italian parsley leaves a handful at a time, processing constantly at high speed until blended. Add $^{3}/_{4}$ cup grated Romano or Parmesan cheese, processing constantly. Store in a covered 1-quart Mason jar in the refrigerator. Use 4 rounded tablespoons of pesto sauce for 1 pound of pasta. You can also mix with equal parts light cream and serve over meat. For variation, try using $^{1}/_{2}$ cup parsley and $^{1}/_{2}$ cup spinach instead of 1 cup parsley. Or, try 1 cup parsley, 1 cup spinach and 1 cup basil instead of 1 cup parsley and 2 cups basil.

Pork Tenderloin in Caper Cream Butter

1 small pork tenderloin, trimmed
2 garlic cloves, minced
3 tablespoons butter, melted
2 ounces capers
2 ounces dry vermouth
1 1/2 cups heavy cream
Salt and white pepper to taste

- Cut the pork into medallions 1/2 inch thick. Flatten the medallions gently to 1/8 inch thick.

- Sauté the garlic in the butter in a large skillet. Add the medallions. Sauté until the medallions are brown. Remove the medallions to a warm plate.

- Add the undrained capers and vermouth to the skillet, stirring to deglaze the skillet. Add the cream. Cook until the mixture is reduced by half. Return the medallions to the skillet. Season with salt and white pepper.

- Cook for 2 minutes or until cooked through. Arrange the medallions on a serving platter and pour the sauce over the top.

YIELD: 6 TO 8 SERVINGS

Roast Tenderloin of Pork with Mustard Wine Sauce

2^{1}/2 pounds pork tenderloin
Salt to taste
2 teaspoons freshly ground pepper
1 teaspoon thyme
2 tablespoons olive oil
1 medium garlic clove, minced
3 medium shallots, minced
^{1}/3 cup dry red wine
1^{1}/2 tablespoons Dijon mustard
1 cup beef stock
5 tablespoons heavy cream
2 tablespoons unsalted butter

• Sprinkle the pork with salt. Press in the pepper and thyme. Sear the pork in the olive oil in a heavy ovenproof skillet over high heat for 3 minutes or until brown.

• Bake at 450 degrees for 16 minutes or until a meat thermometer inserted into the thickest portion registers 160 degrees, turning once. Remove to a cutting board and cover lightly with foil.

• Drain the skillet. Add the garlic and shallots. Sauté over medium-low heat for several minutes or until light brown. Add the wine. Increase the heat to high. Simmer for 1 minute. Stir in the Dijon mustard, stock and cream. Bring to a boil and reduce the heat. Simmer for 6 minutes or until the mixture is reduced to 1 cup. Reduce the heat to low. Stir in the butter.

• Cut the pork into slices and serve with the sauce.

YIELD: 6 TO 8 SERVINGS

Roast Tenderloin of Pork with Orange Glaze

1 (2-pound) pork tenderloin

1 onion, chopped

1 green bell pepper, chopped

1 medium jalapeño chile, seeded and chopped

3 garlic cloves

2 tablespoons chopped fresh cilantro

1 teaspoon oregano

1 tablespoon olive oil

1 tablespoon lemon juice

1/4 teaspoon salt

Juice of 1/2 orange

Juice of 1/2 lemon

2 tablespoons brown sugar

- Rinse the pork and pat dry. Cut small slits in the pork. Purée the onion, bell pepper, jalapeño chile, garlic, cilantro, oregano, olive oil, 1 tablespoon lemon juice and salt in a blender to form a thick paste. Press into the slits in the pork and rub over the entire surface. Place in a sealable plastic bag. Squeeze out the air and seal the bag. Marinate in the refrigerator for 4 to 12 hours.

- Whisk the orange juice, juice from 1/2 lemon and brown sugar in a bowl. Chill, covered, in the refrigerator.

- Remove the pork from the refrigerator and let stand for 30 minutes. Arrange on a rack in a shallow roasting pan.

- Bake at 350 degrees for 45 minutes. Brush with the juice mixture. Bake for 20 to 30 minutes or until the glaze is golden brown and a meat thermometer inserted into the thickest portion registers 160 degrees, basting occasionally with the remaining juice mixture. Let stand for 10 minutes before slicing.

YIELD: 6 SERVINGS

Garlic Rosemary Pork Loin

10 large garlic cloves

2 tablespoons (heaping) rosemary leaves, blanched

1 1/2 tablespoons salt

1 tablespoon freshly ground pepper

1 (4-pound) pork loin, boned and untied

10 whole black peppercorns

1 tablespoon olive oil

- Peel the garlic cloves. Cut each garlic clove into 4 to 6 pieces lengthwise. Combine the garlic, blanched rosemary leaves, salt and ground pepper in a bowl and mix well.

- Place the pork on a board and open out flat with the inside facing up. Spread 1/2 of the garlic mixture over the inside surface. Scatter the whole peppercorns over the top. Roll up the pork. Tie with thread by wrapping the thread around the pork starting at 1 end and pull tight. Do not break the thread but bring it down lengthwise 2 inches and wrap around the pork again. Continue this process until the entire length of the pork is tied with thread every 2 inches or so. Make about 12 punctures 1/2 inch deep in the pork with a thin knife. Fill the holes with most of the remaining garlic mixture. Sprinkle the remaining garlic mixture over the outside surface. Pour the olive oil in a roasting pan. Set the pork in the olive oil.

- Bake at 375 degrees for 1 hour. Turn the pork. Bake for 30 to 35 minutes. Increase the baking temperature to 400 degrees. Bake for 5 to 10 minutes or until brown.

- Remove the pan from the oven. Remove the pork immediately to a serving platter. Let cool for 10 minutes before cutting into thin slices

YIELD: 8 TO 10 SERVINGS

Separating and Peeling Garlic

To separate cloves from a head of garlic, place the blade of a large knife over the head and give it a good smack. To peel a single clove after separation, smack it again and the skins will slide right off.

Honey Dijon Marinated Pork Loin

1/3 cup lime juice

1/4 cup olive oil

1 teaspoon pepper

1/2 teaspoon salt

1/2 teaspoon cumin

2 tablespoons honey

1 tablespoon Dijon mustard

1 teaspoon crushed garlic

1 (11/2-pound) pork loin or tenderloin

- Combine the lime juice, olive oil, pepper, salt, cumin, honey, Dijon mustard and garlic in a bowl and mix well.

- Pierce the pork with a fork. Place in a sealable plastic bag. Add the marinade and seal the bag. Marinate in the refrigerator for 2 hours or longer. Drain the pork, reserving the marinade. Bring the reserved marinade to a boil in a saucepan. Boil for 3 minutes. Place the pork on a grill rack.

- Grill until a meat thermometer inserted into the thickest portion registers 160 degrees, turning and basting periodically with the cooked marinade.

Note: You may also bake at 350 degrees for 30 to 35 minutes or until the pork tests done.

YIELD: 6 SERVINGS

Tip for Measuring Honey

Before measuring honey, spray the measuring spoon or cup with nonstick cooking spray. The honey will slide right off the spoon or out of the cup.

Pork Fricassee with Mushrooms and Carrots

3 tablespoons vegetable oil

3 1/2 pounds boneless pork shoulder, trimmed and cut into 2-inch pieces

1 large onion, chopped

2 ribs celery, chopped

1 bay leaf

4 cups chicken broth

4 cups water

8 carrots, cut diagonally into pieces 1 inch thick

1 pound mushrooms, thinly sliced

1/4 cup (1/2 stick) unsalted butter

1/4 cup flour

1 cup heavy cream

1 tablespoon fresh lemon juice

Salt and pepper to taste

1/2 cup minced fresh parsley leaves

Paprika Rice (page 145)

- Heat the oil in a kettle over medium-high heat until hot but not smoking. Cook the pork in batches in the hot oil until brown, removing the browned pork to a bowl.

- Drain the kettle. Return the pork to the kettle. Add the onion, celery, bay leaf, broth and water. Bring to a boil and reduce the heat. Simmer, uncovered, for 1 1/2 hours or until the pork is tender. Add the carrots. Simmer, covered, for 15 minutes or until the carrots are tender. Remove the pork and carrots with tongs to a bowl. Strain the cooking liquid through a fine sieve, discarding the solids. Return the liquid to the kettle. Boil until the liquid is reduced to 3 cups.

- Sauté the mushrooms in the butter in a large heavy skillet over medium heat until most of the liquid is evaporated. Sprinkle with the flour. Cook over medium-low heat for 3 minutes, stirring to deglaze the skillet. Stir in the cream. Add to the reduced sauce. Simmer until thickened, stirring constantly. Stir in the lemon juice, pork and carrots. Season with salt and pepper to taste. (You may prepare up to 2 days in advance and store, covered, in the refrigerator.) Stir in the parsley just before serving. Discard the bay leaf.

- Serve over Paprika Rice.

YIELD: 10 TO 12 SERVINGS

Crown Pork Roast with Grits Stuffing

1 tablespoon salt

1 tablespoon pepper

2 teaspoons thyme

1 (12-rib) crown pork roast, trimmed

2 cups Grits Stuffing (page 201)

1/4 cup (1/2 stick) butter

1/3 cup flour

2 (14-ounce) cans chicken broth

1/4 teaspoon salt

1/4 teaspoon pepper

• Mix 1 tablespoon salt, 1 tablespoon pepper and thyme together. Rub over the pork. Fold a piece of foil into an 8-inch square. Place on a rack in a roasting pan. Arrange the pork bone ends up on the prepared rack. Bake at 350 degrees for 1 hour.

• Spoon the Grits Stuffing into the center of the pork. Cover with a 12-inch square of foil and fold over the tips of the ribs. Bake for 1 1/2 hours or until a meat thermometer inserted into the center of the pork registers 160 degrees. Remove the foil from the top. Let stand for 15 minutes before slicing.

• Pour the pan drippings into a skillet. Add the butter. Cook until the butter melts. Whisk in the flour until smooth. Cook until caramel colored, whisking constantly. Stir in the chicken broth, 1/4 teaspoon salt and 1/4 teaspoon pepper. Cook until thickened, whisking constantly. Serve with the pork.

YIELD: 8 SERVINGS

Per Serving (excluding unknown items): 89 Calories; 6 g Fat (64.5% calories from fat); 3 g Protein; 5 g Carbohydrate; 16 mg Cholesterol; 1252 mg Sodium. Exchanges: 1/2 Grain (Starch); 0 Lean Meat; 1 Fat.

Grits Stuffing

3 cups water

1^1/$_2$ teaspoons salt

1/4 teaspoon ground pepper

1/2 cup (1 stick) butter

1 cup uncooked grits

1 pound fresh oysters, drained (optional)

1/2 cup grated Parmesan cheese

1 medium red bell pepper, chopped

1 bunch green onions, chopped

3 eggs, lightly beaten

1 cup fine bread crumbs

- Bring the water, salt, pepper and butter to a boil in a large saucepan. Stir in the grits. Return to a boil. Cover and reduce the heat. Simmer for 10 minutes or until the liquid is absorbed, stirring occasionally. Remove from the heat to cool. Stir in the oysters.

- Combine the cheese, bell pepper, green onions, eggs and bread crumbs in a bowl and mix well. Stir into the grits mixture. Use to stuff the Crown Pork Roast on page 200.

Note: For a side dish, spoon the grits mixture into a greased 3-quart baking dish.
Bake at 325 degrees for 45 minutes.

YIELD: 12 CUPS

Per Serving (excluding unknown items): 212 Calories; 11 g Fat (48.4% calories from fat); 8 g Protein; 19g Carbohydrate; 90 mg Cholesterol; 580 mg Sodium. Exchanges: 1 Grain (Starch); 1 Lean Meat; 0 Vegetable; 2 Fat; 0 Other Carbohydrates.

Barbecued Ribs

10 pounds pork ribs

2 teaspoons garlic salt

2 teaspoons pepper

1 tablespoon prepared mustard

1/2 cup chopped onion

2 tablespoons butter or margarine, melted

1/2 cup packed brown sugar

1/4 cup lemon juice

1/4 cup steak sauce

2 tablespoons vinegar

2 tablespoons Worcestershire sauce

1 tablespoon chili powder

- Cut the ribs into serving-size pieces. Arrange in a large Dutch oven and cover with water. Bring to a boil and reduce the heat. Simmer, covered, for 20 minutes; drain well. Sprinkle the ribs with the garlic salt and pepper. Baste with the mustard.

- Sauté the onion in the butter in a saucepan. Add the next 6 ingredients. Simmer for 5 minutes, stirring occasionally. Arrange the ribs in single layers in 3 glass baking dishes and cover with foil.

- Bake at 350 degrees for 1 hour, turning and basting the ribs with the sauce every 20 minutes and removing the foil during the last 20 minutes.

YIELD: 10 TO 12 SERVINGS

Parmesan Breaded Pork Chops

1 cup seasoned bread crumbs

3 tablespoons grated Parmesan cheese

Salt and pepper to taste

1 egg

2 tablespoons milk

8 pork chops

1/2 tablespoon butter or margarine

- Mix the bread crumbs, cheese, salt and pepper in a shallow dish. Beat the egg and milk in a shallow dish. Dip the pork into the crumb mixture, into the egg mixture and then into the remaining crumb mixture to coat. Melt the butter in a baking dish. Arrange the pork in the prepared dish. Bake at 325 degrees for 1 hour or until brown and cooked through, turning after 30 minutes.

YIELD: 4 TO 8 SERVINGS

Mustard Spiced Ham

1 (6-pound) smoked fully cooked ham half, trimmed
1/4 cup Dijon mustard
1/4 cup packed brown sugar
1 teaspoon grated orange zest
1/2 teaspoon ground allspice
1/2 teaspoon ground cinnamon

- Arrange the ham in a roasting pan lined with foil.

- Mix the Dijon mustard, brown sugar, orange zest, allspice and cinnamon in a bowl. Brush some of the mustard mixture lightly over the ham.

- Bake, covered, at 350 degrees for 1 1/2 hours. Uncover and brush the ham with 1/3 of the remaining mustard mixture. Bake, uncovered, for 30 to 45 minutes or until a meat thermometer inserted into the thickest portion registers 140 degrees, basting with the remaining mustard mixture every 10 minutes.

- Remove the ham to a serving platter. Garnish with orange slices and whole cloves.

Note: Lining the baking pan with foil makes cleanup easier.

YIELD: 12 SERVINGS

Arkansas Entertainers Hall of Fame

In 1984, the Arkansas State Legislature passed a bill to set up the Arkansas Entertainers Hall of Fame. Pine Bluff was chosen to be the home of this Hall of Fame. The museum was constructed inside the Pine Bluff Convention Center. The museum opened October 2, 1998, and houses original artifacts from its 26 present inductees. Some of the most notable memorabilia include a $50,000 life-size animatronic statue of Johnny Cash and a Cadillac automobile presented to Cash for his song "One Piece at a Time." Other inductees include: Art Porter, Sr., Lum & Abner, Mary Steenburgen, Al Green, Randy Goodrum, Patsy Montana, Tracy Lawrence, Levon Helm, Harry Thomason, Charlie Rich, Dick Powell, and Wayland Holyfield.

Baked Marinated Ham Steaks

2 (1-inch-thick) ham slices with bone (about 3^1/$_2$ pounds)

^{1}/$_2$ cup port

^{1}/$_2$ cup safflower oil

^{1}/$_4$ cup water

1 garlic clove, crushed

2 bay leaves

6 drops of Tabasco sauce

^{1}/$_2$ teaspoon salt

1 tablespoon fresh lemon juice

^{1}/$_4$ teaspoon freshly ground pepper

^{1}/$_4$ cup Worcestershire sauce

2 tablespoons tomato paste

- Arrange the ham slices in a single layer in a glass baking dish.

- Combine the port, safflower oil, water, garlic, bay leaves, Tabasco sauce, salt, lemon juice, pepper, Worcestershire sauce and tomato paste in a medium saucepan and mix well. Bring to a boil and turn off the heat. Let stand until cool. Pour over the ham.

- Marinate, covered, in the refrigerator for 8 to 12 hours. Return to room temperature.

- Bake at 375 degrees in the marinade for 45 to 60 minutes, turning once. Discard the bay leaves. Cut into serving-size portions.

Note: Great for using up leftover ham after a holiday meal.

YIELD: 6 TO 8 SERVINGS

Sausage and Rice Casserole

1 pound mild bulk pork sausage

8 ounces hot bulk pork sausage

5 green onions with tops, chopped

1 green bell pepper, chopped

1 medium bunch celery and leaves, chopped

2 envelopes chicken noodle soup mix

4$1/2$ cups water

1 cup uncooked brown rice

1 (8-ounce) can sliced water chestnuts, drained

1 package sliced almonds, toasted

- Brown the mild sausage and hot sausage in a skillet, stirring until crumbly. Remove the sausages to paper towels to drain, reserving the drippings in the skillet.

- Sauté the green onions, bell pepper and celery in the reserved drippings in the skillet; drain.

- Cook the soup mix in the water in a saucepan using the package directions. Add the rice, sautéed vegetables and water chestnuts. Stir in the sausage. Spoon into a large greased baking dish.

- Bake, covered, at 350 degrees for 1$1/2$ hours. Sprinkle with the almonds before serving.

Note: Really different and so good.

YIELD: 10 SERVINGS

Herbed Veal with Wine Sauce

2 pounds veal cutlets in 1-inch strips

1/4 cup flour

1/4 cup (1/2 stick) butter

1/4 cup extra-virgin olive oil

Salt and pepper to taste

2 bunches green onions with tops, chopped

3 garlic cloves, chopped

1/4 cup chopped fresh parsley

1 teaspoon Italian herbs

1/4 teaspoon cinnamon

2 cups chicken broth

1 1/4 cups dry white wine

- Dust the veal with the flour. Heat the butter and olive oil in a large skillet over medium-high heat. Add the veal. Cook until brown. Arrange the veal in a 9×13-inch baking dish. Sprinkle with salt and pepper to taste.

- Drain the skillet, reserving 2 tablespoons of the drippings. (If there aren't enough drippings, add additional butter to the drippings to measure 2 tablespoons.) Reduce the heat to medium-low. Add the green onions. Sauté until tender. Add the garlic, parsley, Italian herbs, cinnamon, broth and wine, stirring to deglaze the skillet. Pour over the veal.

- Bake, uncovered, at 350 degrees for 1 hour or until the liquid is reduced. Serve with rice or noodles.

YIELD: 4 SERVINGS

Veal with Artichoke Hearts

2 tablespoons butter

8 ounces veal cutlets

Flour for dusting

2 cups half-and-half or whipping cream

3 tablespoons butter

2 tablespoons tarragon

$1/2$ teaspoon salt

Pepper to taste

1 (10-ounce) package frozen artichoke hearts, cooked and drained

Arrowroot or cornstarch for thickening

- Melt 2 tablespoons butter in a large skillet. Dust the veal with flour. Brown in the hot butter in the skillet. Remove to a plate and keep warm.

- Add the half-and-half, 3 tablespoons butter, tarragon, salt and pepper to the drippings in the skillet over medium-high heat. Stir in the artichokes. Bring to a boil and reduce the heat. Simmer until thickened, adding arrowroot as needed and stirring constantly. Pour over the veal and serve at once.

YIELD: 4 SERVINGS

Apple Brandy Veal Chops

4 veal chops

Salt and pepper to taste

Flour for dredging

3 tablespoons (or more) butter

2 ounces apple brandy

2 ounces white wine

1/2 cup sliced mushrooms

1/2 cup whipping cream

- Season the veal with salt and pepper. Dredge in the flour. Sauté the veal in the butter in a large skillet until brown. Pour the apple brandy over the veal and ignite to flame. Remove the veal to a platter and keep warm.

- Add the wine and mushrooms to the drippings in the skillet. Cook for 2 to 3 seconds. Add the cream. Cook until thickened, stirring constantly. Serve over the veal.

Note: You may use pork chops instead of the veal chops.

YIELD: 4 SERVINGS

Venison Stroganoff

2 pounds venison backstrap or tenderloin

1/3 cup flour

Salt and pepper to taste

2 tablespoons paprika

3 tablespoons vegetable oil

1 cup chopped onion

2 garlic cloves, minced

1 (7-ounce) can mushrooms, drained

1 (10-ounce) can cream of mushroom soup

1 1/2 cups sour cream

- Cut the venison cross grain into 1 1/2-inch strips. Mix the flour, salt, pepper and paprika together. Roll the venison in the flour mixture to coat. Brown in the oil in a skillet. Remove the venison to platter and keep warm, reserving the drippings in the skillet. Add the onion, garlic and mushrooms to the skillet.

- Cook over low heat until the onion is golden brown, stirring to deglaze the skillet. Add the soup. Cook until thickened, stirring frequently. Add the venison. Cook over low heat for 45 minutes or until the venison is tender, stirring frequently. Stir in the sour cream. Heat for 15 minutes. Do not boil. Serve immediately over hot cooked wild rice.

YIELD: 6 SERVINGS

Venison Loin with Grainy Mustard Sauce

2 tablespoons olive oil
1 tablespoon kosher salt
2 tablespoons freshly ground
black pepper
2^1/2 pounds venison,
at room temperature
^{1}/2 cup red wine
1 cup reduced-sodium beef broth
2 tablespoons unsalted butter

1 tablespoon olive oil
1 shallot, minced
2 garlic cloves, minced
^{1}/4 cup grainy mustard
3 tablespoons heavy cream
1 tablespoon canned green
peppercorns, drained (optional)
^{1}/4 teaspoon tarragon, crumbled

- Mix 2 tablespoons olive oil, kosher salt and black pepper in a small bowl to form a paste. Rub the paste on all sides of the venison. Place in a shallow baking pan to allow maximum browning surface.

- Bake at 400 degrees for 25 to 35 minutes or until a meat thermometer inserted into the thickest portion registers between 115 to 120 degrees. Remove from the oven. Cool for at least 15 minutes before slicing.

- Bring the wine and broth to a boil in a heavy saucepan over medium heat. Cook until the mixture is reduced by ^{1}/2. Melt the butter with 1 tablespoon olive oil in a small skillet. Add the shallot and garlic. Sauté for 3 minutes. Combine with the mustard, cream, green peppercorns and tarragon in a small bowl and mix well.

- Whisk 3 tablespoons of the hot wine mixture into the mustard mixture to form a liaison. Return gradually to the hot wine mixture and whisk until smooth. Remove from the heat. Keep warm until ready to serve. (You may reheat in a double boiler.)

- To serve, spoon the sauce over the sliced venison.

YIELD: 6 SERVINGS

Per Serving (excluding unknown items): 394 Calories; 19g Fat (44.8% calories from fat); 47g Protein; 6 g Carbohydrate; 181 mg Cholesterol; 1198 mg Sodium. Exchanges: ^{1}/2 Grain (Starch); 6^1/2 Lean Meat; 0 Vegetable; 0 Non-Fat Milk; 3 Fat.
Nutritional analysis includes the optional ingredient.

Roast Tenderloin of Venison with Cabernet Sauce

2^1/2 pounds venison

2 garlic cloves, minced

Salt and pepper to taste

2 tablespoons olive oil

1^1/2 cups cabernet sauvignon

^{1}/2 cup coarsely chopped shallots

1 small carrot, thinly sliced

1 bay leaf

2 sprigs of fresh Italian parsley

1 cup reduced-sodium beef broth

1 tablespoon unsalted butter

- Rub the venison with the garlic. Sprinkle with salt and pepper to taste. Cook the venison in the hot olive oil in a heavy ovenproof skillet over high heat for 3 minutes or until brown.

- Bake at 450 degrees for 16 minutes or until medium-rare, turning once.

- Bring the wine, shallots, carrot, bay leaf and Italian parsley to a boil in a saucepan over medium heat. Cook for 8 minutes or until the mixture is reduced by ^{1}/2. Strain the mixture, discarding the solids.

- Cook the broth in a saucepan for 7 minutes or until the broth is reduced by ^{1}/2. Add the strained wine mixture and mix well.

- Remove the venison to a cutting board and cover loosely with foil. Drain the skillet, discarding the pan juices. Add the reduced mixture to the skillet, stirring to deglaze the skillet. Whisk in the butter, salt and pepper to taste. Serve with the venison.

YIELD: 6 SERVINGS

Per Serving (excluding unknown items): 358 Calories; 11 g Fat (32.2% calories from fat); 47 g Protein; 6 g Carbohydrate; 166 mg Cholesterol; 158 mg Sodium. Exchanges: 6^1/2 Lean Meat; 1 Vegetable; 1^1/2 Fat.

Venison Swiss Steak

2 pounds venison steaks, cut 1 1/2 inches thick

Flour for dredging

Salt and pepper to taste

Vegetable oil for browning

3 onions, sliced

1 rib celery, sliced

1 cup chopped tomatoes

2 tablespoons Worcestershire sauce

• Dredge the venison in flour. Season with salt and pepper. Brown in enough oil to coat the bottom of an ovenproof skillet. Add the onions, celery, tomatoes and Worcestershire sauce and mix well.

• Bake, tightly covered, at 350 degrees for 1 1/2 hours or until tender.

Note: You may also cook over low heat for 1 1/2 hours or cook in a slow cooker on Low for 8 to 10 hours.

YIELD: 4 SERVINGS

Smothered Venison Chops

6 venison chops
Vegetable oil for browning
$^{1}/_{2}$ cup chicken broth
$^{1}/_{4}$ cup soy sauce
2 tablespoons ketchup
$^{1}/_{4}$ cup honey
$^{1}/_{4}$ teaspoon ginger
1 garlic clove, minced

- Brown the venison in hot oil in a skillet. Combine the broth, soy sauce, ketchup, honey, ginger and garlic in a bowl and mix well. Pour over the venison.

- Cook, covered, over low heat for 30 to 45 minutes or until tender.

YIELD: 6 SERVINGS

Cotton Belt Railroad Engine 819

During the Great Depression, the Cotton Belt Railroad wanted to build 20 new 800 series locomotives. Pine Bluff constructed 10 of these new engines. These were some of the largest steam driven locomotives in the nation. When the new diesel engine came along, the less efficient steam engines were retired and scrapped. One engine, the 819, was spared and presented to the City of Pine Bluff to be displayed in the local park. Since then, the 819 has been restored to its former glory and can be seen today at the Arkansas Railway Museum in Pine Bluff.

Sam's Béarnaise Sauce

1/4 cup tarragon vinegar

1/4 cup dry white wine or vermouth

1 tablespoon (heaping) tarragon

1 tablespoon (heaping) chervil

1 tablespoon (or more) finely chopped shallots

4 egg yolks

1 tablespoon (about) water

1 cup (2 sticks) unsalted butter, softened

Salt and cayenne pepper to taste

- Combine the vinegar, wine, tarragon, chervil and shallots in a double boiler. Cook until the mixture is reduced to a thick paste with just a little liquid remaining. Let cool for about 1 minute.

- Whip the egg yolks and water in a bowl. (This will fluff the egg yolks and give better control while thickening.) Add the egg yolks gradually to the tarragon mixture, stirring constantly.

- Cook until thickened, stirring constantly and being careful not to scramble the egg yolks. Add the butter 2 to 3 tablespoons at a time, stirring constantly. (This can be done on or off the heat.) Season with salt and cayenne pepper.

Note: The sauce can be made an hour or so ahead of time and left at room temperature. The butter and egg yolks can be doubled or use just a little more of the herbs, vinegar and wine. You may omit the salt if using salted butter.

YIELD: ABOUT 2 CUPS

Desserts

Enchanted Land of Lights and Legends

From the third Tuesday in November through New Year's Eve, the Enchanted Land of Lights and Legends beckons one and all to celebrate the magic of the holidays. The Pine Bluff/Jefferson County Regional Park is one of the brightest spots on the planet, with more than seventy displays set up on a mile route that follows the shoreline of Lake Langhofer. This award-winning event is presented by the Pine Bluff Festival Association.

SPONSOR

PINE BLUFF
FESTIVAL ASSOCIATION

Chocolate Swirl Cheesecake

5 tablespoons unsalted butter, melted

2 cups chocolate wafer crumbs

32 ounces cream cheese, softened

1 1/4 cups sugar

5 eggs, at room temperature

2 tablespoons heavy cream

1 tablespoon vanilla extract

3 tablespoons heavy cream

4 ounces semisweet chocolate, finely chopped

- Mix the butter and wafer crumbs in a small bowl. Press in the bottom of a buttered 10-inch springform pan. Bake at 325 degrees for 10 minutes. Remove from the oven to a wire rack to cool.

- Beat the cream cheese at low speed in a large mixing bowl until smooth. Add the sugar gradually, beating constantly. Add the eggs 1 at a time, beating well after each addition and stopping to scrape down the side of the bowl with a rubber spatula several times. Stir in 2 tablespoons cream and vanilla. Pour into the prepared pan. Place on a baking sheet.

- Bring 3 tablespoons cream to a simmer in a small saucepan over high heat. Add the chocolate and reduce the heat to low. Heat until the chocolate melts, stirring constantly. Remove from the heat to cool slightly. Drop by teaspoonfuls onto the top of the batter. Swirl the chocolate mixture into the batter using the tip of a sharp knife to form a decorative pattern.

- Bake at 325 degrees for 1 hour or until the edges are set and the center moves only slightly when the pan is shaken. Turn off the oven. Cool in the oven for 1 hour using a wooden spoon to keep the oven door slightly ajar. Chill, covered, in the refrigerator for 12 hours or longer. Remove from the refrigerator at least 25 to 30 minutes before serving.

YIELD: 15 SERVINGS

Low-Fat Margarita Cheesecake

1 1/4 cups crushed pretzels

1/4 cup (1/2 stick) unsalted butter, melted

24 ounces fat-free cream cheese, softened

2 cups fat-free sour cream

3/4 cup plus 2 tablespoons sugar

3 tablespoons Triple Sec

3 tablespoons tequila

7 tablespoons fresh lime juice

4 eggs

1 tablespoon tequila

1 tablespoon sugar

- Spray a 9-inch springform pan with nonstick cooking spray. Mix the pretzel crumbs and butter in a medium bowl. Press over the bottom and up the side of the prepared pan. Chill in the refrigerator.

- Beat the cream cheese in a large mixing bowl until fluffy. Add 1 1/4 cups of the sour cream, 3/4 cup plus 2 tablespoons sugar, Triple Sec, 3 tablespoons tequila and 5 tablespoons of the lime juice and mix well. Beat in the eggs. Spoon into the prepared pan.

- Bake at 350 degrees on the center oven rack for 50 minutes or until the outside 2 inches are set and the center moves only slightly when the pan is shaken. Remove the cheesecake from the oven and turn off the oven.

- Whisk the remaining 3/4 cup sour cream, remaining 2 tablespoons lime juice, 1 tablespoon tequila and 1 tablespoon sugar in a small bowl until blended. Spread evenly over the cheesecake. Return the cheesecake to the hot oven. Let stand for 45 minutes. (The cheesecake will look very soft but will set when chilled.) Chill in the refrigerator for up to 24 hours.

- To serve, loosen the edge of the cheesecake from the pan with a knife and release the side of the pan. Arrange the cheesecake on a platter. Garnish with lime slices and strips of lime rind.

YIELD: 16 SERVINGS

Per Serving (excluding unknown items): 231 Calories; 5 g Fat (21.2% calories from fat); 11 g Protein; 32 g Carbohydrate; 61 mg Cholesterol; 585 mg Sodium. Exchanges: 1 Grain (Starch); 1 1/2 Lean Meat; 0 Fruit; 1 Fat; 1 1/2 Other Carbohydrates.

Peach Cobbler

1/2 cup (1 stick) unsalted butter

1 cup flour

1 cup sugar

1 tablespoon baking powder

1/8 teaspoon salt

1 cup milk

1 cup sugar

4 cups fresh peaches, sliced

1 tablespoon lemon juice

Ground cinnamon or nutmeg (optional)

- Melt the butter in a 9×13-inch baking dish. Mix the flour, 1 cup sugar, baking powder and salt in a large bowl. Add the milk and stir until the flour mixture is moistened. Pour into the melted butter. Do not stir.

- Bring 1 cup sugar, peaches and lemon juice to a boil in a saucepan over high heat, stirring constantly. Pour over the batter. Do not stir. Sprinkle with cinnamon or nutmeg if desired.

- Bake at 375 degrees for 40 to 45 minutes or until golden brown. Serve warm or cool.

YIELD: 10 SERVINGS

Per Serving (excluding unknown items): 327 Calories; 10 g Fat (27.2% calories from fat); 3 g Protein; 59 g Carbohydrate; 28 mg Cholesterol; 160 mg Sodium. Exchanges: 1/2 Grain (Starch); 1/2 Fruit; 0 Non-Fat Milk; 2 Fat; 2 1/2 Other Carbohydrates.

Band Museum

In 1995, the Band Museum was opened, highlighting the instrument collection of Jerry Horne. It is the only museum in the country dedicated to one-of-a-kind band instruments and the history of the band movement in America. The extensive collection includes instruments owned by the Jimmy Dorsey Band and hometown musician, former band director of Pine Bluff High School, Scrubby Watson. The Band Museum occupies the old Hart Drugstore. This was where Pine Bluff's first Soda Fountain opened in 1890. The more modern 1950s-style Soda Fountain is still operational and is open to the public. The Band Museum and Soda Fountain is open daily from 10:00 a.m.– 4:00 p.m. and Saturday from 12:00 p.m.–4:00 p.m.

Butterscotch Filling

This rich custard filling has a distinctive caramel flavor and is especially good with white or yellow cake. To prepare, combine 1 cup packed dark brown sugar and 1/4 cup (1/2 stick) unsalted butter in a heavy medium saucepan. Cook over low heat until the brown sugar is melted, stirring constantly. Add 1 cup milk and mix well. Continue cooking over low heat. Mix 6 tablespoons flour, 1 teaspoon salt and 1 cup milk in a small bowl until smooth. Whisk into the brown sugar mixture. Cook until thickened, whisking constantly. Whisk in 4 eggs. Cook for 2 minutes. Remove from the heat. Cool for 10 minutes, stirring occasionally. Stir in 1 teaspoon vanilla extract. Cover and chill until needed.

Crème Brûlée

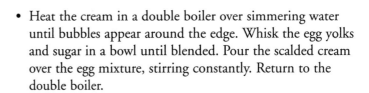

3 cups whipping cream
6 egg yolks
1/3 cup sugar
1 teaspoon vanilla extract
1/3 cup packed brown sugar

- Heat the cream in a double boiler over simmering water until bubbles appear around the edge. Whisk the egg yolks and sugar in a bowl until blended. Pour the scalded cream over the egg mixture, stirring constantly. Return to the double boiler.

- Cook over simmering water until the mixture coats the back of a spoon. (Do not overcook or the custard may curdle.) Remove from the heat. Stir in the vanilla. Pour into an 1 1/2-quart soufflé dish.

- Chill for 8 to 12 hours.

- Sift the brown sugar over the custard. Broil until the brown sugar is melted and bubbly. Chill for 1 to 3 hours before serving.

Note: This is also good served over fruit.

YIELD: 8 TO 10 SERVINGS

Venezuelan Flan

1 (14-ounce) can sweetened condensed milk

1 cup milk

4 eggs

1 teaspoon vanilla extract

1 cup sugar

^{1}/4 cup water

- Beat the condensed milk, milk, eggs and vanilla in a mixing bowl until smooth or process in a blender.

- Cook the sugar and water in a heavy saucepan over medium-high heat for 8 minutes or until the sugar dissolves and becomes golden. Do not stir. Remove from the heat. Pour into a soufflé dish and turn to coat the bottom and side. Pour the condensed milk mixture into the prepared dish. Place in a larger dish. Add enough boiling water to the larger dish to come half way up the side of the soufflé dish.

- Bake at 350 degrees for 1 hour or until a tester inserted into the center comes out clean. Remove the soufflé dish from the water bath and place on a wire rack. Cool to room temperature. Chill, covered, for 8 hours or longer.

- To serve, unmold in a deep serving tray.

YIELD: 6 TO 8 SERVINGS

Watermelon Ice

1 cup sugar

$^3/_4$ cup water

3 to 4 cups chopped seeded watermelon pulp

$^1/_3$ cup lemon juice

- Bring the sugar and water to a boil in a saucepan over high heat, holding the saucepan's handle and swirling the mixture. Cover and boil gently for 4 minutes.

- Purée the watermelon in a blender or food processor. (You should have 2$^1/_2$ cups puréed fruit.) Pour into a stainless steel bowl. Stir in the sugar syrup and lemon juice.

- Freeze, tightly covered, for 4 to 8 hours or until a solid rim of ice forms around the side and the center is partially frozen but not liquid. Whisk until light but not melted. Cover and return to the freezer for 1 hour. Whisk again until light but not melted. Cover tightly and return to the freezer to freeze.

Note: Serve within a few days of preparing for the best flavor. You may also substitute other fruits for the watermelon.

YIELD: 1 QUART

...ate Mousse with Grand Marnier

...l dessert for a dinner party, as it can be prepared fully the night
...nto individual ramekins ready for serving. Fresh orange juice may be
...e Grand Marnier. Make your own candied orange peel or look for
...-quality candied orange peel in specialty food stores.

2 ounces semisweet chocolate

2 tablespoons Grand Marnier

2 eggs, separated

1/8 teaspoon salt

1/4 cup sugar

1/2 cup heavy cream

2 teaspoons candied orange peel (optional)

...colate and liqueur in the top of a double boiler or in a heatproof
...ut not touching simmering water. Heat until melted and smooth,
...Remove from the heat and cool slightly. Whisk in the egg yolks

...s and salt in a mixing bowl until soft peaks form. Add the sugar
...constantly until stiff but not dry peaks form. Stir 1/3 of the
...into the melted chocolate to lighten it. Fold in the remaining

...chilled bowl with chilled beaters until stiff peaks form. Fold into
...ure. Divide evenly among six 6-ounce ramekins. Chill, covered, for
...s or until set. Top with candied orange peel before serving.

...void raw eggs that may carry salmonella, we suggest using
...equivalent amount of pasteurized egg substitute.

YIELD: 6 SERVINGS

...nknown items): 191 Calories; 12 g Fat (55.8% calories from fat);
...hydrate; 90 mg Cholesterol; 51 mg Sodium. Exchanges: 1/2 Lean Meat;
...Other Carbohydrates.
...des the optional ingredient.

Chocolate Raspberry Pots de Crème

2 (10-ounce) packages frozen red raspberries in
light syrup, thawed and drained
1/2 cup whipping cream
1/4 cup sugar
8 ounces semisweet chocolate, broken into pieces
2 egg yolks, at room temperature

- Press the raspberries through a sieve with the back of a spoon, discarding the solids. (You should have 1 cup puréed seedless raspberries.)

- Heat the cream and sugar in a small saucepan over medium-low heat until the sugar is melted, stirring constantly. Bring to a simmer and remove from the heat. Add the chocolate. Cover the pan and let stand for 3 to 4 minutes for the chocolate to soften. Stir until the chocolate is blended into the cream mixture.

- Whisk the egg yolks lightly in a bowl. Add to the chocolate mixture, stirring until the mixture thickens slightly. Add the raspberry purée and mix well.

- Pour into 4 individual ramekins. Chill until ready to serve. Garnish with sliced almonds or fresh raspberries and mint.

Note: You may use one 12-ounce package frozen individual red raspberries.
Save any extra purée and add to Champagne for the perfect raspberry Champagne cocktail.
To avoid raw eggs that may carry salmonella, we suggest using an equivalent
amount of pasteurized egg substitute.

YIELD: 4 SERVINGS

Banana Pudding

3/4 cup sugar

3 teaspoons (heaping) cornstarch

1 cup evaporated milk

1 cup water or milk

2 egg yolks

1 tablespoon butter

1 teaspoon vanilla extract

2 egg whites, at room temperature

1 tablespoon sugar

24 to 30 vanilla wafers

2 medium bananas, sliced

- Bring 3/4 cup sugar, cornstarch, evaporated milk and water to a boil in a saucepan, stirring constantly. Cook until thickened and bubbly, stirring constantly.

- Beat the egg yolks lightly in a bowl. Stir 1/2 of the milk mixture into the beaten egg yolks. Stir the egg yolk mixture into the remaining milk mixture. Cook until thickened, stirring constantly. Remove from the heat. Stir in the butter and vanilla. Chill, covered, in the refrigerator.

- Beat the egg whites in a small mixing bowl until foamy. Add 1 tablespoon sugar gradually, beating until stiff peaks form.

- Layer the pudding, vanilla wafers and bananas 1/2 at a time in a 1-quart glass baking dish. Spread the meringue over the top, sealing to the edge.

- Bake at 425 degrees for 5 minutes or until the meringue is brown.

YIELD: 6 SERVINGS

Chocolate Chunk Bread Pudding with White Chocolate Brandy Sauce

1 (1-pound) loaf dry French bread
3$\frac{1}{2}$ cups milk
1 cup half-and-half
4 eggs, lightly beaten
1 cup sugar
2 tablespoons butter or margarine, melted

1 tablespoon vanilla extract
$\frac{1}{8}$ teaspoon salt
2 (4-ounce) bars Ghirardelli bittersweet chocolate, chopped
White Chocolate Brandy Sauce (below)

- Tear the bread into small pieces into a large bowl. Add the milk and half-and-half. Let stand for 10 minutes. Combine the eggs, sugar, butter, vanilla and salt in a bowl and mix well. Add to the bread and mix well. Stir in the chocolate. Spoon into a lightly greased 9×13-inch baking pan.

- Bake, uncovered, at 325 degrees for 55 minutes or until firm and light brown. Cut into squares and serve warm with White Chocolate Brandy Sauce.

Note: This was served at Charity Ball 2002.

YIELD: 9 SERVINGS

White Chocolate Brandy Sauce

$\frac{1}{2}$ cup sugar
$\frac{1}{2}$ cup (1 stick) butter or margarine
$\frac{1}{2}$ cup half-and-half

1 (4-ounce) bar white chocolate, chopped
3 tablespoons brandy

- Bring the sugar, butter and half-and-half to a boil in a saucepan over medium heat, stirring until the sugar dissolves. Reduce the heat. Simmer for 5 minutes. Remove from the heat.

- Add the white chocolate and stir until the white chocolate melts. Stir in the brandy. Serve warm.

Cold Lemon Soufflé

1 envelope unflavored gelatin

1/4 cup cold water

5 egg yolks

3/4 cup lemon juice

1 tablespoon grated lemon zest

3/4 cup sugar

5 egg whites

3/4 cup sugar

1 cup whipping cream

1/4 cup whipped cream

1 lemon, sliced

- Sprinkle the gelatin over the cold water in a bowl to soften. Mix the egg yolks, lemon juice, lemon zest and 3/4 cup sugar in a double boiler. Cook over boiling water for 8 minutes or until slightly thickened, stirring constantly. Remove from the heat. Add the gelatin mixture and stir until dissolved. Chill, covered, for 30 to 40 minutes.

- Beat the egg whites in a mixing bowl until soft peaks form. Add 3/4 cup sugar gradually, beating constantly until stiff peaks form.

- Beat 1 cup whipping cream in a mixing bowl until stiff peaks form. Fold the egg whites and whipped cream into the lemon mixture. Pour into a 2-quart soufflé dish.

- Chill for 4 hours or longer.

- To serve, dollop with 1/4 cup whipped cream and arrange lemon slices over the top.

YIELD: 8 SERVINGS

Lemon Curd Filling

Whisk 12 egg yolks, 3 tablespoons grated lemon zest, 1 cup fresh lemon juice, 1/2 teaspoon lemon extract and 1 1/2 cups sugar in a medium saucepan. Cook over medium heat for 20 minutes or until thickened and bubbly, stirring constantly with a wooden spoon. Remove from the heat. Add 1 cup butter a small amount at a time, stirring constantly. Chill, covered, for 8 to 12 hours or until firm.

Grand Marnier Soufflé

2 cups milk

$1/2$ cup sugar

$1/8$ teaspoon salt

8 tablespoons flour, sifted

$1/4$ cup cold milk

8 ounces Grand Marnier

12 egg yolks, beaten

2 tablespoons butter, softened

16 egg whites, stiffly beaten

Confectioners' sugar to taste

- Butter 6 small soufflé dishes or ramekins and coat with sugar.

- Bring 2 cups milk, $1/2$ cup sugar and salt to a boil in a saucepan. Blend the flour with $1/4$ cup cold milk in a bowl. Stir into the boiling mixture. Add the Grand Marnier. Cook for 2 to 3 minutes, stirring constantly. Remove from the heat. Add the egg yolks and butter and mix well. Fold in the stiffly beaten egg whites. Pour into the prepared dishes, smoothing the surface.

- Bake at 350 degrees for 20 minutes or until golden brown. Remove from the oven. Sprinkle with confectioners' sugar. Serve immediately.

YIELD: 6 SERVINGS

Per Serving (excluding unknown items): 494 Calories; 17 g Fat (38.0% calories from fat); 19 g Protein; 44 g Carbohydrate; 448 mg Cholesterol; 267 mg Sodium. Exchanges: $1/2$ Grain (Starch); 2 Lean Meat; $1/2$ Non-Fat Milk; 3 Fat; 1 Other Carbohydrates. Nutritional analysis does not include the confectioners' sugar.

Apple Streusel

4 cups sliced peeled apples

1 cup packed brown sugar

$1/2$ cup flour

$1/2$ cup regular or quick-cooking oats

1 teaspoon cinnamon

1 teaspoon nutmeg

6 tablespoons butter or margarine, softened

Whipped cream or ice cream (optional)

- Arrange the apples in a greased 9×13-inch glass baking dish.

- Mix the brown sugar, flour, oats, cinnamon, nutmeg and butter in a bowl until crumbly. Sprinkle over the apples.

- Bake at 325 degrees for 35 to 45 minutes or until the apples are tender and the topping is golden brown.

- Serve warm topped with whipped cream or ice cream.

YIELD: 4 TO 6 SERVINGS

Creamy Custard Filling

This classic custard makes a great filling for cakes or serve as a dessert. To prepare, mix 1 cup sugar, 6 tablespoons flour and $1/4$ teaspoon salt in a small bowl. Heat 2 cups milk in a heavy medium saucepan until hot but not boiling. Pour into the flour mixture and mix well. Return to the saucepan. Cook over low heat for 5 minutes or until thickened and smooth, stirring constantly. Add 4 egg yolks. Cook for 3 minutes, stirring constantly. Remove from the heat. Cool for 10 minutes, stirring occasionally. Stir in 4 teaspoons vanilla extract. Chill, covered, until ready to use.

Apple Cream Cheese Torte

1 cup (2 sticks) butter, softened

2/3 cup sugar

1/2 teaspoon vanilla extract

2 cups flour

8 ounces cream cheese, softened

1/4 cup sugar

1 teaspoon vanilla extract

1 egg

5 to 6 apples, peeled and thinly sliced

1/3 cup sugar

1 teaspoon cinnamon

Dash of lemon juice

1/4 cup sliced almonds

- Cream the butter and 2/3 cup sugar in a mixing bowl until light and fluffy. Add 1/2 teaspoon vanilla and flour and mix well. Press onto the bottom and 3/4 up the side of an 8- or 9-inch springform pan.

- Beat the cream cheese, 1/4 cup sugar, 1 teaspoon vanilla and egg in a mixing bowl until smooth. Pour into the prepared pan.

- Combine the apples, 1/3 cup sugar, cinnamon and lemon juice in a bowl and toss to coat well. Spoon over the cream cheese layer. Sprinkle with the almonds. Push the crust down on the side even with the apple layer using a spoon.

- Bake at 450 degrees for 10 minutes. Reduce the oven temperature to 400 degrees. Bake for 25 minutes or until the center is set.

YIELD: 12 SERVINGS

Espresso Fudge Torte

12 ounces German's sweet chocolate

1^1/2 cups sugar

1^1/2 cups (3 sticks) butter

^{3}/4 cup brewed coffee

6 eggs

1^1/2 cups whipping cream

^{2}/3 cup confectioners' sugar

^{1}/2 teaspoon vanilla extract

- Combine the chocolate, sugar, butter and coffee in a saucepan. Heat until the chocolate melts, stirring constantly. Remove from the heat to cool.

- Beat the eggs in a mixing bowl. Add the chocolate mixture gradually, beating constantly. Pour into a 9-inch springform pan lined with foil.

- Bake at 350 degrees for 40 to 45 minutes or until the cake cracks around the edge and is still soft in the center. Remove from the oven to cool completely. (You may cover and refrigerator for up to 1 week at this point.)

- Whip the cream in a mixing bowl until thick. Fold in the confectioners' sugar and vanilla. Spoon into a pastry bag fitted with a star tip. Pipe on top of the cake. Garnish each serving with chocolate leaves.

Note: This was served at Charity Ball 2000.

YIELD: 12 SERVINGS

Hot Fudge Sauce

1 cup (2 sticks) butter

4^1/2 cups confectioners' sugar

1^1/3 cups evaporated milk

4 ounces unsweetened chocolate

- Melt the butter in a double boiler. Add the confectioners' sugar and evaporated milk. Cook until the confectioners' sugar is dissolved, stirring constantly. Add the chocolate. Cook until smooth, stirring constantly. Continue to cook over hot water for 30 minutes; do not stir. Remove from the heat and stir until smooth and creamy. You may chill and reheat over boiling water before serving. Serve over ice cream or with fruit.

YIELD: 5 CUPS

Mocha Chocolate Trifle

1 (2-layer) package reduced-calorie chocolate cake mix

1 1/3 cups water

2 tablespoons vegetable oil

2 egg whites

1 egg

3 cups skim milk

1 (4-ounce) package fat-free instant chocolate pudding mix

1/2 cup Kahlúa

8 ounces fat-free whipped topping

1/2 cup Hershey's Sweet Escapes, chopped

- Beat the cake mix, water, oil, egg whites and egg at medium speed in a large mixing bowl until blended. Spoon into a 9×13-inch cake pan sprayed with nonstick cooking spray.

- Bake at 350 degrees for 25 minutes or until a wooden pick inserted in the center comes out clean. Cool in the pan on a wire rack for 10 minutes. Remove to a wire rack to cool completely.

- Combine the milk and pudding mix in a medium bowl and mix until smooth and thick.

- Tear the cake into bite-size pieces. Layer the cake, Kahlúa, pudding, whipped topping and chopped candy 1/2 at a time in a 3-quart bowl or trifle dish.

- Chill, covered, for at least 4 hours.

Note: You may substitute strong coffee for the Kahlúa.

YIELD: 16 SERVINGS

Per Serving (excluding unknown items): 242 Calories; 5 g Fat (19.1% calories from fat); 4 g Protein; 42 g Carbohydrate; 13 mg Cholesterol; 336 mg Sodium. Exchanges: 0 Lean Meat; 1/2 Non-Fat Milk; 1 Fat; 2 1/2 Other Carbohydrates.

Easy Strawberry Trifle

2 pints strawberries, cut into halves
2 tablespoons sugar
2 cups whipping cream
4 ounces cream cheese, softened
2 tablespoons sugar
1 pound cake
Melted raspberry jelly
Sherry (optional)

- Combine the strawberries and 2 tablespoons sugar in a bowl and toss to coat.

- Beat the whipping cream in a mixing bowl until stiff peaks form. Beat the cream cheese and 2 tablespoons sugar in a mixing bowl until smooth. Fold into the whipped cream.

- Cut the cake into slices $1/3$ inch thick. Arrange a layer of the cake slices in the bottom of a glass trifle bowl. Sprinkle with 1 teaspoon sherry. Drizzle with melted raspberry jelly. Add a layer of strawberries and a layer of the whipped cream mixture. Repeat the layers, ending with the whipped cream mixture.

- Garnish with 1 or 2 whole strawberries.

YIELD: 16 SERVINGS

Strawberry Sauce

Bring 8 ounces strawberries, 3 tablespoons sugar, $1^1/2$ teaspoons grated orange zest, juice of $1/2$ orange, $1/4$ cup dry white wine and $1^1/2$ teaspoons fresh lemon juice to a boil in a medium saucepan and reduce the heat. Simmer for 5 minutes. Remove from the heat and cover with plastic wrap. Let stand for 10 minutes to allow the favors to infuse. Serve over pound cake.

Carrot Cake with Pecan Cream Cheese Frosting

2 cups flour
1 teaspoon salt
2 teaspoons baking soda
2 teaspoons cinnamon
2 cups sugar
1/2 cup vegetable oil

4 eggs
2 teaspoons vanilla extract
3 cups lightly packed grated carrots
1 cup pecans
Pecan Cream Cheese Frosting (below)

- Sift the flour, salt, baking soda and cinnamon together. Mix the sugar and oil in a mixing bowl. Add the flour mixture and mix well. Add the eggs 1 at a time, beating well after each addition. Beat in the vanilla. Stir in the carrots and pecans. Spoon into a greased and floured large bundt pan or angel food pan.

- Bake at 350 degrees for 45 to 60 minutes or until the cake tests done. Cool in the pan for 10 minutes. Invert onto a wire rack to cool completely.

- Spread Pecan Cream Cheese Frosting over the cake. Store in the refrigerator.

YIELD: 10 TO 12 SERVINGS

Pecan Cream Cheese Frosting

1/2 cup (1 stick) butter, softened
8 ounces cream cheese, softened
1 (16-ounce) package
confectioners' sugar

2 teaspoons vanilla extract
1 cup chopped pecans

- Cream the butter and cream cheese in a mixing bowl until light and fluffy. Add the confectioners' sugar and vanilla and mix until smooth.

- Stir in the pecans.

Chocolate Amaretto Bundt Cake

6 ounces unsweetened chocolate

2 cups flour

1 teaspoon baking soda

1 cup (2 sticks) unsalted butter, softened

1 cup sugar

1 cup packed light brown sugar

4 eggs, at room temperature

1 cup milk

1 tablespoon almond extract

1 teaspoon vanilla extract

1/4 cup amaretto-flavored liqueur

- Melt the chocolate in a double boiler over simmering water over low heat for 5 to 10 minutes, stirring occasionally until smooth. Remove from the heat. Cool for 5 to 10 minutes.

- Sift the flour and baking soda together. Cream the butter, sugar and brown sugar at medium speed in a large mixing bowl for 3 minutes or until fluffy. Add the eggs 1 at a time, mixing well after each addition. Add the chocolate and mix well. Add the flour mixture 1/3 at a time alternating with the milk, almond extract and vanilla extract, beating after each addition until smooth. Add the liqueur and mix well. Pour into a greased and lightly floured 10-inch bundt pan.

- Bake at 350 degrees for 45 to 50 minutes or until a cake tester inserted into the center comes out clean. Cool in the pan for 20 minutes. Invert onto a wire rack to cool completely.

Note: This cake is wonderful by itself or you can top it with Chocolate Glaze on page 237.

YIELD: 16 SERVINGS

Chocolate Buttercream Frosting

Beat 1 cup (2 sticks) unsalted butter, softened, in a medium mixing bowl for 3 minutes or until creamy. Add 4 teaspoons milk and beat until smooth. Add 6 ounces semisweet chocolate, melted, and beat well. Add 1 teaspoon vanilla extract and beat for 3 minutes. Add 1 1/4 cups sifted confectioners' sugar gradually, beating constantly until smooth and creamy.

For Mocha Buttercream Frosting, add 2 to 3 teaspoons instant espresso powder.

Chocolate Kahlúa Cake

1 (2-layer) package chocolate cake mix

1 (4-ounce) package chocolate instant pudding mix

4 eggs

1 cup vegetable oil

$^1/_3$ cup Kahlúa

$^1/_3$ cup vodka

$^1/_2$ cup sugar

$^3/_4$ cup water

$^1/_4$ cup Kahlúa

$^1/_2$ cup confectioners' sugar

- Beat the cake mix, pudding mix, eggs and oil in a mixing bowl until smooth. Add $^1/_3$ cup Kahlúa, vodka, sugar and water and mix well. (The batter will be thin.) Spoon into a greased and floured bundt pan.

- Bake at 350 degrees for 50 minutes or until a wooden pick inserted in the center comes out clean. Cool in the pan for several minutes. Invert onto a serving plate.

- Mix $^1/_4$ cup Kahlúa and confectioners' sugar in a bowl until smooth. Spoon over the warm cake. Let stand until cool.

YIELD: 16 SERVINGS

Double-Chocolate Sour Cream Cake

3 cups plus 2 tablespoons flour

1^1/2 teaspoons baking soda

^{1}/4 teaspoon salt

3 ounces unsweetened chocolate, coarsely chopped

1 tablespoon instant espresso

1^1/2 cups boiling water

^{3}/4 cup (1^1/2 sticks) unsalted butter, softened

2^2/3 cups packed light brown sugar

2 eggs, at room temperature

1^1/2 teaspoons vanilla extract

^{3}/4 cup sour cream

^{2}/3 cup miniature chocolate chips

- Sift the flour, baking soda and salt together. Combine the chocolate, espresso and boiling water in a bowl and stir until the chocolate is melted. Cool for 5 to 10 minutes

- Beat the butter and brown sugar at low speed in a large mixing bowl for 3 minutes or until light and fluffy. Add the eggs 1 at a time, beating well after each addition. Add the vanilla. Add the flour mixture gradually, beating until smooth after each addition. Beat in the sour cream. Add the chocolate mixture ^{1}/3 at a time, beating well after each addition. Stir in the chocolate chips. Pour into a greased and lightly floured 10-inch tube pan.

- Bake at 325 degrees for 70 to 80 minutes or until a cake tester inserted in the center comes out clean. Cool in the pan for 20 minutes. Remove to a wire rack to cool completely.

Note: This cake is wonderful by itself or you can top it with Chocolate Glaze at right.

YIELD: 16 SERVINGS

Chocolate Glaze

Melt 4 ounces semisweet chocolate and ^{1}/4 cup (^{1}/2 stick) butter or cream in a medium saucepan over low heat, stirring occasionally. Remove from the heat. Stir in 1 tablespoon liquor or liqueur of your choice, such as bourbon, rum, Grand Marnier, amaretto, or brandy. Use immediately over completely cooled desserts. Let stand for 15 minutes. You may chill and reheat gently if necessary.

German Chocolate Cake with Caramel Pecan Frosting

4 ounces German's sweet chocolate, broken into squares

1/2 cup water

2 cups flour

1 1/2 teaspoons baking soda

1/4 teaspoon salt

4 egg yolks, at room temperature

1 cup (2 sticks) unsalted butter, softened

2 cups sugar

1 teaspoon vanilla extract

1 cup buttermilk

4 egg whites, at room temperature

1 1/2 (12-ounce) cans evaporated milk

6 egg yolks

1 cup (2 sticks) unsalted butter, cut into small pieces

2 cups sugar

2 teaspoons vanilla extract

4 cups sweetened shredded coconut

2 cups coarsely chopped pecans

- Grease and lightly flour three 9-inch cake pans. Line the bottoms with waxed paper. Melt the chocolate in the water in a small saucepan over low heat, stirring constantly. Remove from the heat and cool for 10 minutes. Sift the flour, baking soda and salt together. Beat 4 egg yolks lightly in a small bowl for 1 minute.

- Beat 1 cup butter and 2 cups sugar at medium speed in a large mixing bowl for 3 minutes or until light and fluffy. Add the egg yolks and beat well. Beat in the chocolate mixture and 1 teaspoon vanilla. Add the flour mixture 1/3 at a time alternately with the buttermilk, beating until smooth after each addition. Beat the egg whites at high speed in a mixing bowl until soft peaks form. Fold into the batter. Spoon into the prepared cake pans.

- Bake at 350 degrees for 25 to 30 minutes or until a cake tester inserted in the center comes out clean. Do not overbake. Cool in the pans for 10 minutes. Remove to wire racks to cool completely.

- Beat the evaporated milk and 6 egg yolks in a large saucepan. Stir in 1 cup butter, 2 cups sugar and 2 teaspoons vanilla. Cook over medium heat for 15 to 18 minutes or until thickened and bubbly, stirring constantly. Remove from the heat. Stir in the coconut and pecans. Spoon into a large bowl. Cool at room temperature for 2 hours or until a good spreading consistency. (The frosting will thicken as it cools.) Spread between the layers and over the top and side of the cake.

YIELD: 12 SERVINGS

Italian Love Cake

1 (2-layer) package fudge marble cake mix

2 pounds ricotta cheese

3/4 cup sugar

4 eggs

1 teaspoon vanilla extract

1 (4-ounce) package chocolate instant pudding mix

1 cup milk

8 ounces whipped topping

- Prepare the cake mix following the package directions. Pour into a greased and floured 9×13-inch cake pan.

- Combine the ricotta cheese, sugar, eggs and vanilla in a mixing bowl and mix well. Spoon over the batter.

- Bake at 350 degrees for 1 hour. Cool in the pan.

- Beat the pudding mix and milk in a mixing bowl until smooth and thick. Fold in the whipped topping. Spread over the cake. Chill, covered, in the refrigerator.

YIELD: 15 SERVINGS

Lemon Buttercream Frosting
Beat 1 cup (2 sticks) unsalted butter, softened, 4 cups confectioners' sugar, 1/2 cup fresh lemon juice and 1 teaspoon grated lemon zest in a large mixing bowl until smooth and creamy. Add 4 cups confectioners' sugar 1 cup at a time, beating until the desired spreading consistency. Add a few drops of yellow food coloring if desired. Use and store at room temperature.

Light Lemon Poppy Seed Cake

1 (2-layer) package reduced-calorie yellow cake mix

1/2 cup sugar

1/3 cup vegetable oil

1/4 cup water

1 cup plain nonfat yogurt

1 cup egg substitute

3 tablespoons lemon juice

2 tablespoons poppy seeds

2 cups confectioners' sugar

1/4 cup lemon juice

- Beat the cake mix, sugar, oil, water, yogurt, egg substitute and lemon juice at medium speed in a large mixing bowl for 6 minutes. Stir in the poppy seeds. Pour into a 10-cup bundt pan sprayed with nonstick cooking spray.

- Bake at 350 degrees for 40 minutes or until a wooden pick inserted in the center comes out clean. Cool in the pan on a wire rack for 10 minutes. Invert onto a wire rack.

- Sift the confectioners' sugar into a bowl. Whisk in the lemon juice gradually until smooth. Drizzle over the warm cake. Cool the cake completely before serving.

YIELD: 24 SERVINGS

Per Serving (excluding unknown items): 195 Calories; 6 g Fat (28.6% calories from fat); 2 g Protein; 33 g Carbohydrate; trace Cholesterol; 84 mg Sodium. Exchanges: 0 Grain (Starch); 0 Lean Meat; 0 Fruit; 0 Non-Fat Milk; 1 Fat; 2 Other Carbohydrates.

Untraditional Birthday Cake

4 cups flour
1 teaspoon baking powder
2 cups (4 sticks) unsalted butter, softened
4 cups sugar
8 egg yolks
2 cups milk
8 egg whites

- Mix the flour and baking powder together.

- Cream the butter and sugar in a large mixing bowl until light and fluffy. Add the egg yolks 1 at a time, mixing well after each addition. Add the flour mixture alternately with the milk, mixing well after each addition.

- Beat the egg whites in a mixing bowl until stiff peaks form. Fold into the batter. Spoon into 4 greased and floured 9-inch cake pans or 5×8-inch loaf pans.

- Bake at 350 degrees for 1 hour or until a cake tester inserted in the centers comes out clean. Cool completely on wire racks before removing from the pans. Frost as desired or serve as a pound cake.

Note: You may reduce the ingredients by half.

MAKES ONE 4-LAYER CAKE OR 4 LOAVES

Seven-Minute Icing
Combine 3 egg whites, $2^1/_4$ cups sugar, $^1/_2$ cup cold water, $1^1/_2$ tablespoons light corn syrup and $^1/_8$ teaspoon salt in a double boiler and place over rapidly boiling water. Beat at high speed for 6 to 8 minutes or until soft peaks form. Remove from the heat. Add $1^1/_2$ teaspoons vanilla extract. Beat for 1 minute or until the desired spreading consistency. Use immediately.

Rum Cake

1 cup chopped pecans
1 (2-layer) package yellow cake mix
1 (4-ounce) package vanilla instant pudding mix
1/2 cup vegetable oil
1/2 cup cold water
1/2 cup light rum
4 eggs
Rum Glaze (below)

- Grease a tube pan. Sprinkle the pecans in the bottom of the pan.

- Combine the cake mix, pudding mix, oil, water and rum in a large mixing bowl and mix well. Add the eggs 1 at a time, beating well after each addition. Pour into the prepared pan.

- Bake at 300 to 325 degrees for 1 hour. Remove the cake from the oven. Pierce holes in the cake using an ice pick. Pour the Rum Glaze over the hot cake. Cool the cake completely before removing from the pan.

Note: This cake freezes well.

YIELD: 16 SERVINGS

Rum Glaze

1 cup sugar
1/2 cup (1 stick) butter
1/4 cup water
1/4 cup rum

- Combine the sugar, butter and water in a small saucepan. Boil gently for 1 minute. Stir in the rum. Let stand for 15 minutes. Use immediately.

Swedish Nut Cake

2 cups sugar

2 cups flour

2 teaspoons baking soda

$1/2$ teaspoon salt

2 eggs

1 (20-ounce) can crushed pineapple

$1/2$ cup pecans

Pecan Cream Cheese Frosting (below)

- Combine the sugar, flour, baking soda, salt, eggs and undrained pineapple in a large mixing bowl and mix well. Stir in the pecans. Spoon into a greased and floured 9×13-inch cake pan.

- Bake at 350 degrees for 30 to 35 minutes or until the cake tests done. Cool slightly. Spread Pecan Cream Cheese Frosting over the warm cake.

YIELD: 15 SERVINGS

Pecan Cream Cheese Frosting

8 ounces cream cheese, softened

$1/2$ cup (1 stick) butter, melted

$13/4$ cups confectioners' sugar

$1/2$ cup pecans

- Beat the cream cheese and butter in a mixing bowl until creamy. Add the confectioners' sugar and mix until smooth.

- Stir in the pecans.

Cream Cheese Icing

Cut 16 ounces slightly softened cream cheese into small pieces. Cut $1/2$ cup (1 stick) slightly softened unsalted butter into small pieces. Beat the cream cheese and butter at medium speed in a medium mixing bowl for 3 minutes or until smooth. Add $11/2$ teaspoons vanilla extract. Add 5 cups sifted confectioners' sugar gradually, mixing well after each addition.

Vanilla Birthday Cake

1 1/2 cups self-rising flour
1 1/4 cups all-purpose flour
1 cup (2 sticks) unsalted butter, softened
2 cups sugar

4 eggs, at room temperature
1 cup milk
1 teaspoon vanilla extract
Vanilla Buttercream Frosting (below)

- Grease and lightly flour three 9-inch cake pans. Line the bottoms with waxed paper. Mix the self-rising flour and all-purpose flour together.

- Cream the butter at medium speed in a large mixing bowl until smooth. Add the sugar gradually, beating constantly for 3 minutes or until fluffy. Beat in the eggs 1 at a time. Add the flour mixture 1/4 at a time alternating with the milk and vanilla, beating well after each addition. Pour into the prepared cake pans.

- Bake at 350 degrees for 20 to 25 minutes or until a cake tester inserted in the centers comes out clean. Cool in the pans for 10 minutes. Invert onto wire racks to cool completely. Spread Vanilla Buttercream Frosting between the layers and over the top and side of the cake.

YIELD: 12 SERVINGS

Vanilla Buttercream Frosting

1 cup (2 sticks) unsalted butter, softened
8 cups confectioners' sugar

1/2 cup milk
2 teaspoons vanilla extract

- Combine the butter, 4 cups of the confectioners' sugar, milk and vanilla in a large mixing bowl and beat until smooth and creamy. Add the remaining confectioners' sugar 1 cup at a time, beating constantly until the desired spreading consistency. (You may not need all of the remaining confectioners' sugar.)

- Use at room temperature since the frosting will set if chilled. You may store in an airtight container at room temperature for up to 3 days.

Note: You may tint with food coloring, if desired.

Watergate Cake

1 (2-layer) package white cake mix

3/4 cup vegetable oil

3 eggs

1 cup 7-Up

1 (4-ounce) package pistachio instant pudding mix

1 cup finely chopped pecans

1/2 cup shredded coconut

Watergate Frosting (below)

1/2 cup shredded coconut

3/4 cup finely chopped pecans

- Combine the cake mix, oil, eggs, 7-Up, pudding mix, 1 cup pecans and 1/2 cup coconut in a large mixing bowl. Beat for 3 minutes. Pour into a greased and floured bundt pan.

- Bake at 350 degrees for 45 minutes. Cool in the pan for 10 minutes. Invert onto a wire rack to cool completely. Frost with Watergate Frosting. Sprinkle with 1/2 cup coconut and 3/4 cup pecans.

YIELD: 8 TO 10 SERVINGS

Watergate Frosting

2 envelopes whipped topping mix

1 1/2 cups milk

1 (4-ounce) package pistachio instant pudding mix

- Combine the whipped topping mix, milk and pudding mix in a large mixing bowl and beat until thick and smooth.

Martha Mitchell
Martha Beall Mitchell was born on September 2, 1918 in Pine Bluff, Arkansas. She married Attorney General John Mitchell who was later appointed U. S. Attorney General by President Richard M. Nixon. Martha Mitchell is well known in U.S. history for being outspoken about the Watergate scandal during the Nixon administration. After her death in 1976, a section of Highway 65, which runs through Pine Bluff, was renamed in her honor, the Martha Mitchell Expressway.

Cream Cheese Brownies

1 (2-layer) package butter pecan or yellow cake mix
1/2 cup (1 stick) butter, melted
1 egg
3 1/2 cups confectioners' sugar
8 ounces cream cheese, softened
1/2 cup (1 stick) butter, melted
2 eggs
Coarsely chopped pecans

- Mix the cake mix, 1/2 cup butter and 1 egg in a bowl. Press into a greased 9×13-inch cake pan.

- Combine the confectioners' sugar, cream cheese, 1/2 cup butter and 2 eggs in a mixing bowl and mix until smooth. Pour into the prepared pan. Sprinkle with pecans.

- Place in a cold oven. Bake at 300 degrees for 55 minutes. Cool completely before serving.

YIELD: 15 SERVINGS

Chocolate Chip Icing

For a quick sheet cake or cookie icing, sprinkle some chocolate chips on top and pop into a hot oven for a minute or two or until the chocolate chips are softened. Remove from the oven and spread over the top.

Heath Bar Brownies

Piece of butter for coating

3/4 cup pecan halves or pieces (2 1/2 ounces)

5 (1 1/4-ounce) Heath candy bars, or 20 miniature Heath candy bars

1/2 cup (1 stick) unsalted butter

2 ounces unsweetened chocolate

2 eggs

3/4 cup sugar

1/2 teaspoon vanilla extract

1/4 teaspoon salt

1 cup sifted unbleached flour

- Turn an 8×8-inch baking pan upside down. Press a 12-inch sheet of foil shiny side down onto the pan, shaping it to the sides and corners with your hands. Remove the foil. Run tap water into the pan until wet all over. Pour out all but 1 tablespoon water. Place the shaped foil into the pan and press gently against the sides and bottom.

- Melt a piece of butter in the prepared pan on the bottom oven rack in a 350-degree oven. Remove from the oven. Spread over the foil using a piece of crumpled plastic wrap. Spread the pecans in a shallow baking pan. Bake for 12 minutes or until very hot.

- Cut the candy bars crosswise into slices 1/4 to 1/3 inch thick. (You should have about 1 1/2 cups.) Chop a scant 1/4 cup of the candy bars into smaller pieces. Melt 1/2 cup butter and unsweetened chocolate in a double boiler over warm water, stirring occasionally. Remove from the heat to cool slightly.

- Beat the eggs, sugar, vanilla and salt at medium speed in a medium mixing bowl until smooth. Add the melted chocolate and beat just until mixed. Add the flour. Beat at low speed until mixed. Stir in the toasted pecans and candy bar slices with a wooden spoon. Spread the batter in the prepared pan. Sprinkle with 1/4 cup chopped candy bars. Bake at 350 degrees for 28 minutes or until a wooden pick inserted in the center comes out just barely clean. Cool in the pan on a wire rack.

- Cover the pan with a flat board or baking sheet and invert. Remove the pan and peel off the foil. Cover the brownie layer with a piece of parchment paper or waxed paper. Top with another board or baking sheet and invert again so the brownie layer is right side up. Chill for 1 hour. Cut the brownie layer into quarters. Cut each quarter into halves so you will have 8 strips. Cut each strip crosswise into 3 equal portions. Serve at room temperature or chilled

YIELD: 24 SMALL BROWNIES

Chocolate Chip Cookies

1¹/₂ cups unsifted flour

1 teaspoon salt

1 teaspoon baking soda

1 cup shortening

1 cup packed light brown sugar

1¹/₂ cups sugar

1 teaspoon vanilla extract

2 eggs

2 cups old-fashioned oats

2 cups (12 ounces) semisweet chocolate chips

- Mix the flour, salt and baking soda together on waxed paper.

- Beat the shortening, brown sugar, sugar and vanilla in a large mixing bowl until creamy. Add the eggs and beat until light and fluffy. Beat in the flour mixture and oats gradually. Stir in the chocolate chips.

- Drop by well-rounded teaspoonfuls onto greased cookie sheets.

- Bake at 350 degrees for 8 to 10 minutes or until golden brown. Cool on the cookie sheets for 2 minutes. Remove to wire racks to cool completely.

YIELD: 7¹/₂ DOZEN

Triple-Chocolate Cookies

$1/2$ cup shortening

$1/2$ cup (1 stick) butter or margarine, softened

$3/4$ cup sugar

$3/4$ cup packed brown sugar

1 teaspoon baking soda

2 eggs

1 teaspoon vanilla extract

2 ounces unsweetened chocolate, melted and cooled

$1/4$ cup baking cocoa

2 cups flour

8 ounces semisweet chocolate or

white chocolate baking squares, broken into chunks

- Beat the shortening and butter at medium-high speed in a large mixing bowl for 30 seconds. Add the sugar, brown sugar and baking soda and beat until combined. Beat in the eggs, vanilla and melted chocolate. Beat in the baking cocoa and as much of the flour as possible with the electric mixer. Stir in any remaining flour with a wooden spoon. Stir in the semisweet chocolate.

- Drop by rounded tablespoonfuls 2 inches apart onto ungreased cookie sheets.

- Bake at 375 degrees for 8 to 10 minutes or until the tops look dry. Cool on the cookie sheets for 1 minute. Remove to wire racks to cool completely.

Note: You may use one 10-ounce package white chocolate baking pieces for the chocolate.

YIELD: 4 DOZEN

Lemon Bars Deluxe

2 cups flour

¹/2 cup confectioners' sugar

1 cup (2 sticks) butter, softened

¹/4 cup flour

¹/2 teaspoon baking powder

4 eggs, beaten

2 cups sugar

¹/3 cup lemon juice

Confectioners' sugar to taste

- Sift 2 cups flour and ¹/2 cup confectioners' sugar into a bowl. Cut in the butter until the mixture clings together. Press into a greased 9×13-inch baking pan. Bake at 350 degrees for 25 to 30 minutes or until light brown.

- Sift ¹/4 cup flour and baking powder together. Beat the eggs, sugar and lemon juice in a mixing bowl. Stir in the flour mixture. Pour over the baked layer. Bake for 25 to 30 minutes or until set. Cool in the pan on a wire rack. Sprinkle with confectioners' sugar to taste and cut into bars.

YIELD: 3 DOZEN

Lemon Cream Cheese Cookies

1 cup (2 sticks) butter, softened

3 ounces cream cheese, softened

1 cup sugar

1 egg yolk

¹/2 teaspoon lemon juice

1 teaspoon grated lemon zest

2¹/2 cups sifted flour

¹/2 teaspoon salt

Colored sugar (optional)

Finely chopped nuts (optional)

- Cream the butter, cream cheese and sugar in a mixing bowl until light and fluffy. Add the egg yolk, lemon juice and lemon zest and mix well. Beat in the flour and salt. Place the dough in a cookie press fitted with a star tip. Press onto greased cookie sheets. Bake at 350 degrees for 15 minutes or until golden brown. Sprinkle with colored sugar and nuts. Cool on wire racks.

Note: You may shape the dough into balls and flatten onto cookie sheets.

YIELD: ABOUT 2 DOZEN

Peanut Butter Cookies

1 1/2 cups sifted flour
1 teaspoon baking soda
1/2 cup shortening
1/2 cup sugar

1/2 cup packed brown sugar
1 egg
1/2 cup peanut butter

- Sift the flour and baking soda together. Melt the shortening in a large microwave-safe bowl. Add the sugar and brown sugar and beat well. Beat in the egg. Add the peanut butter and beat well. Stir in the flour mixture.

- Shape into 1-inch balls. Arrange on ungreased cookie sheets. Flatten with a fork. Bake at 350 degrees for 10 to 12 minutes or until golden brown.

YIELD: ABOUT 2 DOZEN

Praline Cookies

1 cup packed light brown sugar, sifted
1 tablespoon flour
1/2 teaspoon salt

1 tablespoon rum
1 egg white, beaten
2 cups large pecan halves

- Combine the brown sugar, flour, salt and rum in a large bowl. Fold in the beaten egg white. Fold in the pecans.

- Arrange each coated pecan half back side down on cookie sheets sprayed with nonstick cooking spray.

- Bake at 300 degrees for 30 minutes. Remove from the cookie sheets immediately to cool.

YIELD: AS MANY COOKIES AS PECAN HALVES

Traditional Iced Sugar Cookies

8 cups sifted flour

2 tablespoons baking powder

2 teaspoons salt

$2^2/3$ cups shortening

3 cups sugar

4 eggs

2 teaspoons vanilla extract

2 teaspoons grated orange zest

$1/2$ cup milk

8 cups confectioners' sugar

$1/2$ cup (1 stick) butter, softened

$2/3$ cup evaporated milk

2 tablespoons pure vanilla extract

- Sift the flour, baking powder and 1 teaspoon of the salt together. Cream the shortening and sugar in a mixing bowl until creamy. Add the eggs and beat until light and fluffy. Add the vanilla and orange zest and mix thoroughly. Stir in the flour mixture and $1/4$ cup of the milk.

- Divide the dough into 2 equal portions. Chill, covered, for 1 hour or until the dough is easy to handle. Roll 1 portion at a time $1/8$ inch thick, keeping the remaining portion in the refrigerator until ready to use. Cut into desired shapes with cookie cutters. Arrange 2 inches apart on greased cookie sheets.

- Bake at 375 degrees for 12 minutes. Cool on wire racks. Combine the confectioners' sugar, butter, remaining salt, evaporated milk, remaining milk and vanilla in a large mixing bowl and beat at high speed until smooth. Spread on the cookies.

YIELD: 8 DOZEN

Family Tradition

When our first child was old enough to sit in a high chair, my husband and I started a tradition of making and decorating cookies for every holiday. As each additional child arrived, we made room until there were six of us making cookies and memories around the table.

The table was my grandmother's old oak library table to which we added a large marble top. It became known as the "cookie table" and is one of our most cherished possessions.

Forty-five years later, we continue the tradition of cookie making and decorating with grandchildren and great-grandchildren.
—Von Talbot

Sesame Seed Cookies

1 cup (2 sticks) butter, softened
1¹/2 cups sugar
1 teaspoon vanilla extract
3 eggs
5 cups self-rising flour, sifted
¹/2 teaspoon cinnamon
¹/2 cup sesame seeds
1 egg
2 tablespoons milk

- Cream the butter in a large mixing bowl until light. Add the sugar and vanilla and beat well. Add the eggs 1 at a time, beating well after each addition. Add the flour and cinnamon and mix to form a soft dough.

- Chill, covered, for 3 to 12 hours.

- Roll a scant tablespoonful of the dough into a rope 3¹/2 inches long. Pinch the ends together to form a doughnut shape. Dip in the sesame seeds. Repeat with the remaining dough and sesame seeds.

- Arrange several inches apart on greased cookie sheets. Brush with a mixture of the egg and milk.

- Bake at 375 degrees for 15 minutes or until light brown. Cool on wire racks. Store in an airtight container.

YIELD: 6 DOZEN

3$1/2$ cups flour

1 teaspoon baking soda

1 teaspoon salt

1 cup (2 sticks) butter, softened

1 cup sugar

1 cup light brown sugar

1 egg, lightly beaten

1 cup vegetable oil

1 teaspoon vanilla extract

1 cup rolled oats

1 cup crushed cornflakes

$1/2$ cup flaked coconut

$1/2$ cup chopped pecans

Sugar for coating

- Sift the flour, baking soda and salt together. Cream the butter and 1 cup sugar and brown sugar in a mixing bowl until light and fluffy. Add the egg, oil and vanilla and mix until blended. Add the flour mixture and mix well. Stir in the oats, cornflakes, coconut and pecans.

- Shape into $3/4$-inch balls. Roll in sugar to coat. Arrange 2 inches apart on ungreased cookie sheets. Press with a moistened fork.

- Bake at 350 degrees for 10 to 12 minutes or until golden brown. Cool on the cookie sheets for a few minutes. Remove to wire racks to cool completely.

Note: In memory of Catherine O. Seabrook.

YIELD: 10 TO 12 DOZEN

Pralines

2 cups pecan halves	1 tablespoon butter
2 cups sugar	1/2 cup sugar
1 cup half-and-half	1 teaspoon vanilla extract

- Prepare a workspace in your kitchen for beating the hot candy and dropping onto waxed paper.

- Remove any shells or bitter pieces from the pecans. Arrange the pecans on a baking sheet. Bake at 325 degrees for 8 minutes or until toasted. Remove from the oven.

- Bring 2 cups sugar, half-and-half and butter to a boil in a heavy saucepan. Melt 1/2 cup sugar in a cast-iron Dutch oven or large heavy saucepan until a caramel color, rolling the sugar around in the pan or using a wooden spoon to stir if needed. Watch carefully to prevent burning. Add the cream mixture and stir with a wooden spoon until smooth. Add the pecans.

- Cook over medium heat to 235 degrees on a candy thermometer, soft-ball stage. (The soft-ball stage is when you can form a soft ball between your fingers when you drop a little of the hot candy mixture in a cup of cold water.) Remove from the heat and set on a heavy pad. Let stand for 1 minute.

- Stir in the vanilla with a wooden spoon. Beat for 3 to 5 minutes or until the mixture thickens and cools slightly. A light haze will begin to form on the top of the mixture. Drop onto waxed paper to harden. As the pralines harden, gently pull the waxed paper to make sure it is not sticking to the countertop. When the pralines are completely cool, the waxed paper can be removed easily.

Note: If, for some reason, your candy does not harden, then do the next best thing. Place all the soft candy in a heavy saucepan and reheat adding a little rum. You'll have the best praline sauce for ice cream that you've ever tasted.

YIELD: 2 DOZEN (3-INCH) PRALINES OR 3 DOZEN (2-INCH) PRALINES

English Butter Toffee

1 cup sugar

1 cup (2 sticks) unsalted butter

$1/4$ cup water

$1/2$ teaspoon salt

1 teaspoon vanilla extract

$1/2$ cup slivered almonds

- Butter a 10×15-inch baking sheet or piece of parchment paper. Combine the sugar, butter, water and salt in a heavy saucepan.

- Bring to a boil over medium-high heat, stirring constantly until the sugar is dissolved. Cook to 305 degrees on a candy thermometer, hard-crack stage, stirring occasionally. Remove from the heat.

- Stir in the vanilla and almonds. Pour onto the prepared baking sheet. Let stand until cool. Cut or break into pieces. Store in an airtight container.

YIELD: 1 POUND

Crème Fraîche

Combine 2 tablespoons buttermilk and 2 cups whipping cream in a bowl and blend well. Let stand at room temperature for 6 to 8 hours. Cover and chill for at least 24 hours before using or serving.

Apple Crumb Pie

1/4 cup sugar	Flaky Pastry for Two-Crust Pie (below)
1 tablespoon flour	2 1/4 cups flour
1 1/2 teaspoons cinnamon	1 1/2 cups unpacked light brown sugar
3 cups sliced peeled tart apples,	1 cup (2 sticks) unsalted butter,
such as Granny Smith	softened, cut into small pieces

- Mix the sugar, 1 tablespoon flour and cinnamon in a large bowl. Add the apples and toss gently to coat. Line a 9-inch pie plate with 1/2 of the Flaky Pastry, trimming and fluting the edge. Spoon the apple mixture into the prepared pie plate.

- Mix 2 1/4 cups flour and brown sugar in a medium bowl. Cut in the butter with a pastry blender until crumbly. Sprinkle over the apple mixture until covered. Bake at 425 degrees for 10 minutes. Reduce the oven temperature to 375 degrees. Bake for 25 to 35 minutes longer or until golden brown on top. Serve warm with ice cream, if desired.

Note: You may top with the remaining Flaky Pastry instead of the crumb topping, if you prefer.

YIELD: 6 TO 8 SERVINGS

Flaky Pastry for a Two-Crust Pie

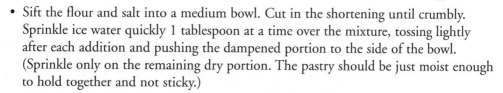

2 cups sifted flour	3/4 cup shortening
1 teaspoon salt	4 to 5 tablespoons ice water

- Sift the flour and salt into a medium bowl. Cut in the shortening until crumbly. Sprinkle ice water quickly 1 tablespoon at a time over the mixture, tossing lightly after each addition and pushing the dampened portion to the side of the bowl. (Sprinkle only on the remaining dry portion. The pastry should be just moist enough to hold together and not sticky.)

- Use for a 2-crust pie or to line two 9-inch pie plates. Bake at 425 degrees for 12 to 15 minutes or until light brown.

YIELD: ENOUGH PASTRY FOR 2-CRUST PIE OR 2 PIES

Blue Ribbon Buttermilk Pie

3 eggs

1 1/4 cups sugar

1/2 cup buttermilk

1/4 cup (1/2 stick) margarine, melted

1 teaspoon vanilla extract

1/16 teaspoon salt

1 unbaked (9-inch) pie shell

- Beat the eggs, sugar, buttermilk, margarine, vanilla and salt in a mixing bowl until smooth. Pour into the pie shell. Bake at 350 degrees for 40 to 50 minutes or until light brown.

YIELD: 6 TO 8 SERVINGS

Deep-Dish Chocolate Chip Pie

2 eggs

1/2 cup packed brown sugar

1/2 cup sugar

1/2 cup (1 stick) butter or margarine, melted

1/2 cup flour

1 cup (6 ounces) chocolate chips

1 cup pecan pieces

1 unbaked (10-inch) deep-dish pie shell

- Beat the eggs, brown sugar, sugar and butter in a mixing bowl until blended. Add the flour and beat until smooth. Stir in the chocolate chips and pecan pieces. Pour into the pie shell. Bake at 350 degrees for 45 minutes.

Note: It's great served warm with ice cream.

YIELD: 6 TO 8 SERVINGS

French Silk Chocolate Pie

1/2 cup (1 stick) butter, softened

3/4 cup sugar

1 square unsweetened chocolate, melted

1 teaspoon vanilla extract

2 eggs, chilled

1 baked (9-inch) pie shell

8 ounces whipping cream, whipped

1/4 cup slivered almonds, toasted

- Cream the butter and sugar in a mixing bowl until light and fluffy. Add the chocolate and vanilla and mix well. Add the eggs 1 at a time, beating for 2 minutes after each addition. Pour into the baked pie shell.

- Chill for 1 hour. Top with whipped cream and toasted almonds.

Note: To avoid raw eggs that may carry salmonella, we suggest using an equivalent amount of pasteurized egg substitute.

YIELD: 6 TO 8 SERVINGS

One-Crust Pie Pastry

Cut 1/2 cup shortening into 1 1/3 cups flour with a pastry blender in a large bowl until crumbly. Sprinkle 3 tablespoons ice water 1 tablespoon at a time over the mixture until moistened, tossing constantly with a fork. Shape into a ball. Roll into a 10-inch circle on a lightly floured surface. Fit into a 9-inch glass pie plate, trimming and fluting the edge. Bake at 425 degrees for 10 minutes or until light brown.

Favorite Cream Pies

3/4 cup sugar

1/3 cup flour, or 3 tablespoons
cornstarch

1/4 teaspoon salt

2 cups milk

3 egg yolks, lightly beaten

2 tablespoons butter

1 teaspoon vanilla extract

1 baked (9-inch) pie shell, cooled

3 egg whites

1/2 teaspoon vanilla extract

1/4 teaspoon cream of tartar

6 tablespoons sugar

- Mix 3/4 cup sugar, flour and salt in a saucepan. Stir in the milk gradually. Cook over medium heat until bubbly, stirring constantly. Cook for 2 minutes longer. Stir a small amount of the hot mixture into the egg yolks. Stir the egg yolks into the hot mixture. Cook for 2 minutes, stirring constantly. Remove from the heat. Stir in the butter and 1 teaspoon vanilla. Pour into the cooled baked pie shell.

- Beat the egg whites in a mixing bowl until soft peaks form. Add 1/2 teaspoon vanilla and cream of tartar. Add 6 tablespoons sugar gradually, beating constantly until stiff and glossy peaks form and all of the sugar is dissolved. Spread over the hot filling, sealing to the edge.

- Bake at 350 degrees for 12 to 15 minutes or until the meringue is brown. Remove from the oven to cool.

- VARIATIONS: For *Chocolate Cream Pie,* prepare the vanilla filling as above, increasing the sugar to 1 cup. Chop 2 ounces unsweetened chocolate and add with the milk. *For Coconut Cream Pie,* add 1 cup flaked coconut to the vanilla pie filling. Sprinkle the meringue with 1/3 cup coconut before baking. *For Butterscotch Cream Pie,* substitute brown sugar for the sugar in the vanilla pie filling and increase the butter to 3 tablespoons. *For Banana Cream Pie,* cut 3 bananas into slices. Layer in the baked pie shell and pour the vanilla pie filling over the top.

Note: Dip the knife into water before cutting a meringue-topped pie.

YIELD: 8 SERVINGS

Lemon Chiffon Pie

1 envelope unflavored gelatin

3 tablespoons cold water

4 egg yolks

1/2 cup sugar

Juice of 1 lemon

Grated lemon zest

4 egg whites

1/2 cup sugar

1 baked (9-inch) pie shell

1 cup whipping cream

1 tablespoon sugar

1 teaspoon vanilla extract

- Soften the gelatin in the cold water in a small bowl for 15 minutes.

- Beat the egg yolks in a mixing bowl until creamy. Add 1/2 cup sugar, lemon juice and a small amount of lemon zest and mix well. Pour into a double boiler. Cook until thickened, stirring constantly. Remove from the heat. Stir in the gelatin.

- Beat the egg whites in a mixing bowl until soft peaks form. Add 1/2 cup sugar gradually, beating constantly until stiff peaks form. Fold into the custard mixture. Pour into the baked pie shell. Chill in the refrigerator.

- Whip the whipping cream, 1 tablespoon sugar and vanilla in a mixing bowl until stiff peaks form. Spread over the top of the pie, sealing to the edge. Chill until ready to serve.

YIELD: 6 TO 8 SERVINGS

Creamy Pecan Pie

8 ounces cream cheese, softened

1/3 cup sugar

1/4 teaspoon salt

1 teaspoon vanilla extract

1 egg

1 unbaked (9-inch) deep-dish pie shell

1¼ cups chopped pecans

1/4 cup sugar

1 cup light corn syrup

1 teaspoon vanilla extract

3 eggs

- Combine the cream cheese, 1/3 cup sugar, salt, 1 teaspoon vanilla and 1 egg in a mixing bowl and beat until smooth. Pour into the pie shell. Sprinkle with the pecans.

- Combine 1/4 cup sugar, corn syrup, 1 teaspoon vanilla and 3 eggs in a mixing bowl and beat until smooth. Pour over the pecan layer. Bake at 375 degrees for 35 to 40 minutes or until set.

YIELD: 6 TO 8 SERVINGS

Peppermint Pie with Rice Krispies Crust

4 ounces German's sweet chocolate

1/4 cup (1/2 stick) margarine

3 cups Rice Krispies

1/2 gallon vanilla ice cream, softened

3/4 cup crushed peppermint candy

- Break the chocolate into pieces into a heavy saucepan. Add the margarine. Heat until melted, stirring constantly. Remove from the heat. Add the cereal and mix well. Press in the bottom and up the side of a 10-inch pie plate. Chill in the refrigerator.

- Mix the ice cream and peppermint candy in a bowl. Spoon into the prepared pie plate. Freeze for 3 to 4 hours or until firm.

YIELD: 6 TO 8 SERVINGS

Double-Layer Pumpkin Pie

4 ounces cream cheese, softened

1 tablespoon milk

1 tablespoon sugar

16 ounces whipped topping

1 (9-inch) graham cracker pie shell

1 (16-ounce) can pumpkin

2 (4-ounce) packages vanilla instant pudding mix

1 teaspoon cinnamon

1/2 teaspoon ginger

1/2 teaspoon nutmeg

1 cup milk

- Whisk the cream cheese, 1 tablespoon milk and sugar in a large bowl until smooth. Stir in 1 1/2 cups of the whipped topping. Spread into the pie shell.

- Whisk the pumpkin, pudding mix, cinnamon, ginger, nutmeg and 1 cup milk in a large bowl until smooth. Spread over the cream cheese layer.

- Chill for 4 hours. Serve with the remaining whipped topping.

YIELD: 6 TO 8 SERVINGS

Contributors

Janice Acosta
Martha Allison
Catherine Anne Atkinson
Susan Attwood
Diane Ayres
Layne Baugh
Kathie Beavers
Melinda Becker
Gail Bellingrath
Alicia Bratton Bigger
Linda Black
Lauren Bland
Janelle Blue
Bill Brabston
Sandra Breshears
Helen Claire Brooks
Belinda Brown
Laura Brown
Pat Brown
Susan Talbot Brown
Jaynie Cannon
Kelly Casada
Barbara Cash
Denise Castleberry
Cari Cates
Gary Lynn Cheatham
Susan Cheesman
Tammy Claussen
Leigh Cockrum
David Cook
Lisa Cook
Joannye Crabb
Robin Banks Dawson
Carol Dedman
Sue DeMaine
Claudette Dixon
Mike Drewett
Cindy Dunn
Melanie Edmonson

Rebecca Edwards
Sarah Faust
Cheryl Fox
Mildred Franco
Bonnie Fratesi
Nancy Fuller
Sharon Garner
Jennifer Graves
Peggy Harris
Brenda Hawkins
Lori Heird
Claire Holmes
Jason Hornsby
Laura Beth Hornsby
Amanda Howerton
Debbie Howorka
Shirley Hubanks
Dorothea Jacque'
Paige Smith Jernigan
Meredith Hagan
Jodie Jolly
Pam Jones
Vicki Juneau
Rick Kientz
Nick Kines
Mary Ann Kizer
Eric Klein
Tori Rogers Klein
Erin Koenig
Lisa Kosmitis
Vicki Krupala
Cathy Lewis
Pat Lile
Beverly Brainard Madison
Cindy May
Lynette McAliney
Tankie McFall
Nancy McNew
Jamie McNulty

Michealle Minyard
Melinda Montgomery
Frances Moore
Cappi Morgan
Kelli Norman
Susan Norton
Debbie Ogg
Nancy Oudin
Marybeth Passmore
Linda Payne
Eleanor Pearce
Evelyn Pearce
Leigh Pearce
Linda Petterson
Kelly Pittman
Lisa Price
Michelle Price
Elizabeth Reddin
Amy Reed
Sue Reed
Cathy Reid
Floradel Reid
Casey Riemenschneider
LaNelle Roberts
Norma Roberts
Susan Roberts
Virginia Robinson
Ann Rogers
Susan Sanders
Kayla Santaella
Sandrine Schroeder
Jay Scriber
Virginia Scriber
Alisa Secrest
Chuck Seel
Valla Seel
Corinne Shepherd
Marcia Shultz
Simply the Best Catering

Joanne Smith
Moppy Smith
Sue Smith
Misti Smykla
Kim Soto
June West Spakes
Phyllis Speer
Kelly Spence
Jane Starling
Beverly Ann Stevens
Susan Stobaugh
Heather Stone
Keith Sutton
Von Talbot
Wendy Talbot
Chris Taylor
Jamie Terrell
Pollye Tharp
Lisa Thrash
Lala Treviño
Treviño Specialty Foods
Ann Brown Turner
Carolyn Turner
Arlene Tyler
Neely Ursery
Dawn Waddle
Andy Wagstaff
Cindy Wagstaff
Heather White
Renee White
Sonya White
Jan Whitlock
Selma Wineland
Dena Witt Woerner
Ellen Burks Wyatt
Christy Young
Melissa Young

Bibliography

Leslie, James W.,

Land of Cypress and Pine, More Southeast Arkansas History,

Rose Publishing Company, Inc., 1976.

Leslie, James W.,

Pine Bluff and Jefferson County, A Pictorial History,

Rose Publishing Company, Inc., 1981.

Leslie, James W.,

Saracen's Country, Some Southeast Arkansas History,

Rose Publishing Company, Inc., 1974.

Index

266

Southern Accent
A Second Helping

The Junior League of Pine Bluff, Inc.
P.O. Box 1693
Pine Bluff, Arkansas 71613-1693
870-535-5027 phone
870-535-0181 phone/fax
888-568-2665 (COOK)

Name

Street Address

City   State   Zip

Telephone

YOUR ORDER	QTY	TOTAL
Southern Accent, A Second Helping at $24.95 per book		$
Southern Accent at $16.95 per book		$
Shipping & handling at $3.50 for first book, $1.50 for each additional book, or only $10.00 for six books.		$
	TOTAL	$

Method of Payment: [   ] MasterCard   [   ] VISA   [   ] AmEx   [   ] Discover
[   ] Check enclosed payable to the *Southern Accent*

Account Number   Expiration Date

Cardholder Name

Signature

Photocopies accepted.